MW00561853

Asking Better Questions

Teaching and Learning for a Changing World

JULIANA SAXTON

CAROLE MILLER

LINDA LAIDLAW

JOANNE O'MARA

3rd edition

Pembroke Publishers Limited

© 2018 Pembroke Publishers
538 Hood Road
Markham, Ontario, Canada L3R 3K9
www.pembrokepublishers.com

Distributed in the U.S. by Stenhouse Publishers
www.stenhouse.com

All rights reserved.
No part of this publication may be reproduced in any form or by any means electronic or mechanical, including photocopy, scanning, recording, or any information, storage or retrieval system, without permission in writing from the publisher. Excerpts from this publication may be reproduced under licence from Access Copyright, or with the express written permission of Pembroke Publishers Limited, or as permitted by law.

Every effort has been made to contact copyright holders for permission to reproduce borrowed material. The publishers apologize for any such omissions and will be pleased to rectify them in subsequent reprints of the book.

Funded by the Government of Canada
Financé par le gouvernement du Canada | Canadä

Ontario
Ontario Media Development Corporation
Société de développement de l'industrie des médias de l'Ontario

Library and Archives Canada Cataloguing in Publication

Saxton, Juliana, author
    Asking better questions : teaching and learning for a changing world /
Juliana Saxton, Carole Miller, Linda Laidlaw, Joanne O'Mara. -- Third edition.

First and second editions written by Norah Morgan and Juliana Saxton.
Includes index.
Issued in print and electronic formats.
ISBN 978-1-55138-335-4 (softcover).--ISBN 978-1-55138-935-6 (PDF)

    1. Questioning. 2. Teaching. 3. Learning. I. Miller, Carole, 1943–, author
II. Laidlaw, Linda, author III. O'Mara, Joanne, author IV. Morgan, Norah,
1918–. Asking better questions. V. Title.

LB1027.44.M67 2018   371.102   C2018-903291-X
                                          C2018-903292-8

Editor: Kate Revington
Cover Design: John Zehethofer
Typesetting: Jay Tee Graphics Ltd.

Printed and bound in Canada
9 8 7 6 5 4 3 2 1

MIX
Paper from
responsible sources
FSC® C004071
www.fsc.org

Contents

Appendixes *100*

Acknowledgments

The journey of *Asking Better Questions* from first edition to this third edition has benefited from the support and encouragement of our colleagues and students, national and international. Many generous invitations to work with students, faculty, and local teachers have resulted in a new edition that reflects a wider context. Participants have contributed their knowledge and understanding of a world undergoing vast changes. We are so grateful to them.

We would like to thank particularly Dr. John O'Toole, who has remained steadfast in his support of our work; Dr. Robyn Ewing, University of Sydney; Dr. John Saunders, Sydney Theatre Company; Dr. Ross Prior, University of Manchester; Dr. David Dynak, Westminster College, Utah; Dr. Peter O'Connor, University of Auckland; and the many organizations that have provided time and space for us to present our ideas to a broader audience.

The inclusion of the Ann Graham inquiry has been central to each edition, and for this we are grateful to Dr. Jonothan Neelands, University of Warwick. Excerpts from ICARUS AT THE EDGE OF TIME by Brian Greene, copyright © 2008 by Brian Greene are used by permission of Alfred A. Knopf, an imprint of the Knopf Doubleday Publishing Group, a division of Penguin Random House LLC. All rights reserved. Excerpt from TRAIN TO SOMEWHERE by Eve Bunting. Text © 1996 by Eve Bunting. Reprinted by permission of Clarion Books, an imprint of Houghton Mifflin Harcourt Publishing Company. All rights reserved. *Six Pack Shame*, the central image for Chapter 11, is by Australian award-winning quilt artist, Linda Steele. We thank her for permission to use this provocative piece of fabric art.

We have been privileged to work once again with Kate Revington, our patient editor, and continue to be amazed by her thoughtful and inquisitive additions and emendations to the text — we are becoming better writers thanks to her tactful suggestions. As always, Mary Macchiusi, a publisher beyond compare, was able to envision the possibilities of a third edition; we are so appreciative of our long association together.

In the preparation of this text, we were constantly reminded of the late Norah Morgan. Thinking of her brilliant mind, allied to her superb teaching abilities, challenged us to keep students, participants, teachers, and facilitators at the forefront of our writing.

Foreword: The Mercurial Character of Contemporary Questions

There is something beautifully open about questions. Questions have a modesty about them; *we do not always have answers.* Questions imply curiosity; *we are keenly interested.* Questions beget more questions; *we grow and evolve through inquiry.* Questions can transport people into new imaginings and into new ways of thinking.

But questions can also bedevil and confront us. *Where were you? What are you doing? How old are you?* Questions like these can make people feel uncomfortable, maybe even scared. So, one cannot be naïve about the power of questions.

It is more pressing than ever for young people to be equipped with critical understandings about questions and asking the right types of questions, not only in relation to the questions people ask, but also in the *how, when, why,* and *where* that people ask them.

People ask questions for a whole range of reasons: to find information, to be polite, to probe more deeply. I am reminded of Leo Tolstoy's story "The Three Questions" when young Nikolai asks: When is the best time to do things? Who is the important one? And, what is the right thing to do?* These questions strike me as bigger life issues or inquiries that can be asked at different points in life. They lie somewhere between questions that shape understandings and questions that call for reflection.

What screens, social media, and even emails have ushered in are ways of asking questions without eye contact and contextual cues — these are mediums that allow for all kinds of deception and anonymity. Honing the art of questioning and listening attentively has never been more foundational to being informed and educated.

In this book, the authors carefully and intelligently offer three categories of questions: questions that elicit information; questions that shape understandings; and questions that press for reflection. In this third edition of *Asking Better Questions,* what the authors excel at is moving questioning and inquiry into a digital age which begs its own set of questions: How are questions different now compared with the past? Through what mediums do we ask our big questions? And to what degree are the answers real, fake, or embellished?

One could say that there has never been a greater need to put "facts" to the test and ask the right questions.

Jennifer Rowsell
Canada Research Chair in Multiliteracies
Brock University

---

* "The Three Questions" appears in Leo Tolstoy, *What Men Live By and Other Tales,* translated by Louise and Aylmer Maude (2011). The original work was published in 1885.

Introduction: Engaging with Things That Matter

The 2006 edition of *Asking Better Questions* simply acknowledged the advent of the digital age and an interest in inquiry-based curricula, but in the years since, there have been some extraordinary transformations for those of us who teach and learn. In a world moving so swiftly that it hardly leaves us time to think, now, more than ever, we need to provide students and participants, as well as their teachers and facilitators, with better and more varied kinds of questions. Doing so will enable them to unlock the deeper meanings of their complex environments. Furthermore, the ways in which we access, process, and create information through new technologies offer different conditions for, and challenges to, that thinking.

In this book, we offer readers opportunities to develop their questioning skills and to examine how they might enable students to take on a more critical stance through questioning and acting on the answers they find. Our hope is that this new edition not only reframes familiar strategies and techniques but also introduces ways of working that address media opportunities and enhance the processes of student-centred inquiry.

Information technologies have become so pervasive that recent research has shown that, for many young people, there is no distinction between being online and offline (Carrington 2017). Very young children are using digital tools and practices and, although physically in the material world, they are also moving "seamlessly across online and offline spaces, such as playing with toys that are connected to the internet" (Marsh et al. 2017, 3). These changes disrupt pedagogical practices and change learning dispositions, yet many of the pedagogical models for teaching practices and the physical conditions of learning in school remain 20th century constructs. As Robin Goodfellow (2014) points out, "critical judgment and the truth value of knowledge continues to dominate much teaching and most assessment practice, even in contexts where new subjects and new means of communication are reshaping the curriculum" (11).

The Role of Questions in Developing Critical Awareness

Goodfellow's assessment, inevitably, drives us to ask further questions that lead us to the central theme of this new edition: How do we help our students develop an ethical stance that supports and sustains them in a "post truth" world? How do we help them consider critical and reflective questions, so that they may better sort out their political, social, economic,

The *Oxford Dictionaries* define *post-truth* as what happens in a world in which "objective facts are less influential in shaping public opinion than appeals to emotion and personal belief." The online resource recognized *post-truth* as its international Word of the Year 2016.

The Key Question Driving This Text

How can we encourage deep learning, support the exploration of meanings, and generate engaged conversations about things that matter?

and personal worlds? How do we help students and participants, novice teachers, facilitators, as well as seasoned educators, develop the necessary knowledge, skills, and strategies to "distinguish 'spin,' 'truthiness,' 'fake news' and the 'my facts are as good as your facts' rationalization of somebody's subjective views of reality" (Johnson 2018, A8)? As Ronald Vale (2013) puts it, "the most important skill for the 21st century . . . is learning how to judge and integrate information from multiple sources to generate conceptual understanding or a new idea" (4).

As authors, we recognize that the readers of this text will be working in a variety of contexts. Some will have well-funded extensive computer access and classroom sets of laptops and iPads; others will work with limited or no technological resources. For many people, technological resources are non-existent; instead, safety, nourishment, and shelter are of primary importance. Whatever the situation, what we present depends only on a commitment to explore the driving question of this text: How can we encourage deep learning, support the exploration of meanings, and generate engaged conversations about things that matter?

For most people, asking questions is a direct way to discover information and to learn how people think and feel about many topics, issues, and matters of interest. But in some cultures, question-asking may be viewed as challenging the power of an authority figure or what peers are saying in a discussion. As a result, participants may prefer a more conversational or storying approach.

It is important, therefore, to be mindful of these differences when creating the kinds of safe environments necessary for critical, empathic, and reflective talk. As suggested in a British Columbia Aboriginal education document (n.d.) from School District No. 22, facilitators and teachers need "to be aware of the 'agency' of participants and the hierarchy of power relations that influence the ways participants may experience the situation, and whether they will be able to join in" (69). As in any teaching context, we must be clearly aware of our own reasons for emphasizing the importance of asking questions and questioning answers as much for ourselves as for the students we teach.

Several ideas presented in this resource were first explored by us in *Drama, Theatre and Performance Education in Canada: Classroom and Community Contexts* (Miller and Saxton 2015). As drama teachers we work in classrooms in which social justice, respect, and a sense of self are the media through which students engage in discussions, conversations, and chat. Race, status, culture, privilege and oppression, access and exclusion, competition and collaboration, differences and similarities, domination and empowerment, as well as all manner of states of in-betweenness, represent some of the content explored and questioned through drama. We recognize that, for many, this is also the content of any number of classes and that the issues of today's curricula in project-based, inquiry learning models are much the same.

What Enables Effective Questioning

Regardless of the discipline, questioning is at the heart of whatever we teach, and we must acknowledge that effective learning — and teaching —

When we think, "[w]e don't just speed a thought through our neural networks — we inhale it, hold it, wait for it to send ripples through the whole of our being." — Sven Birkerts (1995, chapter 10, n.p.)

takes time. This time for thinking enables critical thought and allows for consideration of both thinking and feeling. Time is what allows for reflection. It enables students and participants to see the shape of their own identities come more clearly into focus. We seem unable to make time, and yet it is time that creates the space for making effective questions.

The means of nurturing critical thinkers lies in the ability of teachers, facilitators, and students to ask the sorts of questions that develop thoughtful reasoning, invite reflection, and promote the ability to assess, appraise, and criticize. We have always known that. Today's profoundly complex world also demands the ability to deconstruct patterns of meaning. Yet the digital component raises a concern. While offering a convenient, personalized, and much richer multimodal landscape it can — without intentional guidance or the exercise of a more critical eye — encourage a kind of broad grazing that generates its own learning demands. This often comes at the expense of a critical ear, eye, and heart.

A Reflection of Contemporary Understandings

This third edition reflects changes in curriculum design. Here, we include more integrative examples that embrace digital ways of learning as well as the more traditional means. Where appropriate, we have updated the material; however, we have retained the framework for creating questions because it remains valid. We build on the research, scholarship, ideas, strategies, and lessons offered in 2006 while recognizing that digital media have changed our understanding of how to communicate. Furthermore, this third edition explicitly recognizes that contemporary classrooms are increasingly diverse culturally, linguistically, and ethnically.

Here, in brief, is what this text does:

- It includes opportunities for teachers and students to explore content through digital media. It does so by building on students' interests and capacities for complexity and change, and their facility with media.
- It presents our research on the use of conditional language (I wonder if it's possible . . . ?) to enhance discussion, dialogue, deliberation, and conversation through effective questions (see Chapter 5).
- It recognizes the reality of a change in classroom dynamics. Today Google, Siri, Alexa, our peers, and digital contacts may have as many answers as the teacher.
- It addresses recent concerns on the loss of empathy due to a lack of ability to connect face to face.
- It recognizes a paradox. A digital world is typically two-dimensional, but we live our lives in a three-dimensional physical and social context. That means we have a responsibility to find ways to mediate healthy accommodations.
- Finally, it offers strategies and techniques for finding the means to move beyond the comfortable echo chambers of sites that hold only ideas with which we are already familiar and comfortable.

In summary, this new text is written within a critical literacy framework that acknowledges that technology can play a role as a medium for learning. It focuses on an understanding of cultural contexts with attention to the power dynamics, conflicting perspectives, unwritten assumptions, and biases inherent in most of the materials taught and accessed. We begin with a brief historical overview that highlights past pedagogical thinking and how it resonates with current educational changes.

Chapter 1   Setting the Context

Freire's *Pedagogy of the Oppressed*, first published in 1968, began to influence northern hemisphere educators only when Donaldo Macedo joined with Freire to introduce critical pedagogy to the wider world. Their text, *Literacy: Reading the Word and the World*, was first published in 1987. Freire's influential ideas underpin our work with questions in this book.

"Authentic education is not carried on by 'A' *for* 'B' or by 'A' *about* 'B' but rather by 'A' *with* 'B.'" That recognition is at the heart of Paulo Freire's pedagogy, presented in *Pedagogy of the Oppressed* (1970, 70). Freire's pedagogy "brings teachers, parents and students together around new and more emancipatory visions of community" (Giroux 1987, 9). His acknowledgment of relationships as central to effective teaching is as relevant today as it was 50 years ago.

In Freire's method and practice of teaching, classes examine current issues through communal discussion and reflection. The pedagogy relies on asking the kinds of questions that take us below the surfaces of the world we are making. "Criticism, for Freire," writes Ann Berthoff (1987), "always means interpreting one's interpretations, reconsidering contexts, developing multiple definitions, tolerating ambiguities so that we can learn from the attempt to resolve them" (xviii–xix).

Questioning as an Act of Citizenship

Freire's critical, constructivist, and socialist utopian philosophy, it must be admitted, is still mainly to be found in post-degree courses in faculties of education. Nevertheless, the need to ask the kinds of uncomfortable questions that a true democracy requires of its citizens is more important today than ever. It is not an "easy style of life — to have the courage to risk, to stand up, to question, to think deeply," John Ralston Saul (1995) notes; however, it is the "primary weapon in the exercise of our legitimacy" (169). But the "art of question-making" that Neil Postman (1979) identified as "one of the central disciplines in language education" (140) continues to be neglected.

Why? Eric Booth (1999) provides one answer: "We are answer-oriented everywhere, having been trained to this through schooling that is almost entirely *right-answer* driven" (103). Booth also observes that "[s]cant notice is ever given to the *quality* of our questions." Other likely reasons lie in the fact that people shy away from asking uncomfortable questions, and in the 600-year-old tradition of the *sage on the stage*, there exists a hierarchy based on tacit agreement between students and teachers.

Educational Practices in Revolutionary Times

"Social intelligence has become ripe for rethinking as neuroscience begins to map the brain areas that regulate interpersonal dynamics."
— Daniel Goleman (2006, 83)

The past decades have been a revolutionary time for education at all levels, but much of what we are discovering is, unfortunately, not yet being applied in educational contexts. As researchers discover how the brain works, we have learned that feelings are important to cognition; we have also discovered their importance as a means of creating long-term memory. (See, for example, Caine and Caine 1994; Damasio 1999, 2003; and Frederickson 2001.) Yet how well do our school programs reflect this?

A wide array of school programs and supports recognize the value of social and emotional learning (SEL) with an emphasis on the ethical aspects of that learning (Cohen 2006). However, such programs and supports tend to focus on providing students with coping mechanisms and competencies. They may address the stresses of being in school but not the root causes of those stresses.

At the same time, the value of emotional and social connections to learning has not led to confirming the importance of the arts as a learning medium. Instead, there is an imbalance. The privileging of STEM (Science, Technology, Engineering, Mathematics) has resulted in a subsequent lessening of the place of the arts and humanities as part of a holistic curriculum (Laird 2010). We observe with interest recent holistic shifts in understanding the relationships across the sciences, arts, and humanities. There is now a focus on STEAM (Science, Technology, Engineering, Arts, Math) and the "maker" movement, which embraces creative problem-solving, blending hands-on learning through technology, craft, science, and literacy (Halverson and Sheridan 2014).

Nel Noddings (2002, 23) affirms, "Caring about is empty if it does not culminate in caring relations." All curricula, therefore, are built upon the developing relationship between student and teacher.

The tension between traditional practices and progressive education is increasing. What Booth (1999, 103) describes as the "high-demand, quick-fix nature of our lives" places new stresses on learning and teaching. Over recent decades, across international contexts, the rise of the back-to-basics curriculum, with its standards and high-stakes testing, has been vigorously opposed by those who understand that "big ideas" should drive curriculum (Wasserman 2007) and that teaching and learning can be a "curriculum of ethical care" (Noddings 2005). Curriculum theorist William Doll (1993/2008) reminds us that traditional curriculum is a closed system: it "can only *transfer*." Open systems, on the other hand, are, "by their very nature, *transformative*: rich, rigorous, recursive and relational" (1993, 7).

The major technology corporations provide models of transformational systems. The kind of open approach Doll identifies permeates the ways in which these corporations present themselves. They promote imagination and creativity as important attributes for those seeking employment. In Project Oxygen, Google conducted a detailed analysis of all the hiring, firing, and promotion data that they had collected since their incorporation in 1998. Not surprisingly to us, they found the following:

> The seven top characteristics of success at Google are all soft skills: being a good coach; communicating and listening well; possessing insights into others (including others' different values and points of view); having empathy toward and being supportive of one's colleagues; being a good

critical thinker and problem solver; and being able to make connections across complex ideas. (Strauss 2017, n.p.)

However, on the education front, thinking — especially critical thinking — at all levels has, in many cases, become a victim of curricula of expediency and outcomes, and perhaps teacher uncertainty about how to proceed with developing critical skills.

Outside educational institutions, the world has been telling us for years that we must deal with what Homer-Dixon (2001) calls the widening "ingenuity gap." Doing so requires an agenda for curricula not so much different in their *content* as in *how* that content is conveyed, made use of, and reflected upon. That kind of content delivery — which is as old as Plato — Freire (1970) called "problem-posing education." Today we call it "inquiry-based learning." Although challenging and exciting, inquiry-based learning offers curricula that, for many, remain fraught with risk. Nonetheless, we are entering an era where education authorities worldwide are revisiting and revising approaches and programs of study to acknowledge new frames for learning. One key frame is competency-based instruction, which shifts away from objectives and an emphasis on content. Perhaps we may see ingenuity gaps begin to narrow . . .

Putting Students' Questions at the Centre

Good teaching "places students' questions, ideas and observations at the centre of the learning experience . . . moving [them] from a position of wondering to a position of enacted understanding and further questioning" (Scardamalia 2002, 2). That positioning is beginning to happen even as the teaching and learning climate seems to become chillier. But talking about change does not effect change. We must make a concerted effort to bring about what we know in our hearts is necessary to effect positive change.

Today our universities and colleges, schools, and preschools are filled with learners from different countries, backgrounds, socio-economic statuses, and cultural traditions, and with diverse abilities. Diversity can (and should) enrich our teaching, challenging each of us to find new ways of exploring content. As is the case in ecological contexts, diversity will lead to more robust, complex systems.

One of those ways of exploring content is to revisit and revision that oldest of instructional techniques: how questioning works and how it can work better. This brief update on contemporary influences on classroom practice has looked at why shifting that practice meets such resistance and demands so much effort.

In Chapter 2, we consider the influences on education brought about by "the digital revolution" in communication through technologies.

Chapter 2   Questioning in a Rapidly Changing World

In this chapter, we consider the place and necessity of questioning in our rapidly changing world.

Technology: Its Unrealized Promises

You may remember the original hype around information and communication technologies: these advances would accomplish the tedious, time-consuming labors of thought (data collection, computation, research, and so on). Through automated reasoning, it was supposed, humans would have more time to think deeply and reflectively about "the unfolding of human creativity" (Turkle 2015, 76).

There was also the promise that, with everyone on computer, we would enter a "paperless world" which, along with tidier desks and empty waste-paper baskets, would have a gratifyingly ecological vision of vast forests saved from clear-cutting. The reality has been that initially many people used more paper, as they printed out emails and copies of everything they wished to save. Only much more recently has paper use in offices declined.

Early descriptions of the Internet were framed with a romantic philosophy. The Internet was "a force for peace in the world" that could, through its worldwide communications embrace, build "a common global community" of "shared understanding" of the problems that confront us all (Foer 2017). Instant connections to thousands, even millions of people would make criticism, resistance, and revolution possible; this intensely responsive network would make democracy easier by helping citizens to challenge authority.

Today we see many examples: people using social media to organize, to build community, and to protest and work together for change. We have seen police brutality through citizens' videos, known of government documents leaked and spread through social media, and heard from victims of violence as they come forward to share their stories. The Internet, and the social media it hosts, has delivered the promise of providing a way of sharing; what we still lack, however, is the shared understanding of problems that confront us all and, indeed, a commitment to striving for the common good.

An Expanded View of Literacy

In thinking through the impact of information and communication technologies, we pose Hilary Janks's (2012) question for critical literacy: "Whose interests are being served?" To expand on it we can also ask: Who benefits? Who does not? What might be the principles and ethics of those writers, and how might they fit into our own views of the world? These questions need to be addressed.

In terms of our classrooms, following tectonic shifts in digital technologies, we have an expanded view of literacy: one that provides us with new understandings of what makes a text (Honan 2012). The multimodal nature of digital text encourages us to view images, symbols, signs, and sounds as valid ways of interpreting information that is democratic, accessible, and non-elitist. Digital technologies enable alternative ways of accessing information in order to demonstrate understanding and collaborate with peers. New digital technologies can also "even the playing field" for children who struggle to get the words down or otherwise have difficulties with literacy or numeracy (Laidlaw and O'Mara 2015). Some students, even among those struggling with words or numbers, are extremely knowledgeable and facile with technology. They can often be seen helping teachers to navigate their devices, thus offering a power shift: teacher as learner and student as teacher.

The world of information to which technology allows access provides a way of seeing with new perspectives. Much of what had to be described orally or through two-dimensional pictures is now at our fingertips. Words, people, history, and current events can be shared in the here and now and across borders and continents. Digital media provide groups with many opportunities to create original projects that demand soft skills, such as collaboration, cooperation, sharing of responsibilities, and the development of digital etiquette. New digital media have much to offer and multiple ways of creating new opportunities for learning. By 2015, researchers began to accept the fact that "digital technologies were here to stay . . . and the question became how best to engage with mobile devices" (Katz 2016).

Linda Laidlaw and Suzanna Wong affirm that technology can be transformative if children are not seen as passive viewers but as active producers and creators of content (personal communication, 2018). This idea resonates with Paulo Freire's critical pedagogy.

The Need to Exercise Critical Literacy

The ability to self-publish and share means that a broader range of views is published than ever before. For teachers, this means spending more time developing questioning skills in our students. Doing so can allow them to develop what we call "the librarian in the head," an actively aware approach to reading online. In the past when students needed information about a topic, they would head to the library. There the librarian would help them select material from resources that the school had chosen. Now students will typically go online for information. Some information is more extensive, useful, and well researched than anything students were previously able to access; other information, however, may be incorrect, incomplete, or supporting extreme perspectives.

Consider this example. As authors, we have worked extensively with *Rose Blanche*, a fictional text written by Christophe Gallaz and illustrated by Roberto Innocenti. The story is set during the Second World War at the time of the Holocaust. It affords a good opportunity for students to conduct research. Teachers could send students to the library to research the setting or ask the librarian to prepare a box of books about the Holocaust. Or, students could go online for information. Some of the resources students can access are far better and more extensive than those available in most school libraries. That research, however, can be problematic. The range of materials accessed may not be age appropriate or factually accurate; more concerning is that students can easily access materials written by extremist groups, including Holocaust deniers. That uncensored material highlights the importance of developing thoughtful reasoning in students so that they can become critically literate, independent thinkers.

Our new ability to obtain a seemingly endless stream of information can mean that we spend less time thinking about what we have discovered and instead become distracted by other things. Who of us has managed to avoid going down the rabbit holes of information? That distracted attention is nothing more than the old survival habit of curiosity at work. In addition, the image capabilities of digital media have become so commonplace that there is a growing tendency to spend as much (or more) time recording our life experiences as we do having them.

We accept that there is no way of putting the genie back in the bottle, nor would we want to. But if we are to provide ways to embrace technology without losing our humanity, we must be aware of areas of concern and address potential problems.

The Digital Reality

Sherry Turkle (2015), a professor of social sciences and technology, has, for the last 30 years, studied the relationship between the use of digital media and its effects on those who use it. Turkle suggests that screen-based media may deepen loneliness because the devices provide a way to hide behind physical and social interactions. As well, when we are engaged in viewing digital media, we are always looking at something distanced from us, revealed to us by a set of algorithms: "invisible lines of code on distant servers" (Sax 2015, A10).

Algorithms, put into place by human beings, are procedures that not only "get the job done" but solve problems at incredible speeds. They are great for certain things. Are we not pleased to be able to access these resources? But the world we live in is not separated from us by a device. It is here and now; it is complex, ambiguous, open always to change. Our relationship to the world and to each other is existential and constitutive; in other words, we are making it happen, and it is happening to us. We and the world are always in a state of "becoming," to use Maxine Greene's word (Pinar 1998). Although old problems may be solved, there are always new problems and the need for new procedures and innovations for which no algorithms have yet been invented.

Attention grabbers

In this contingent world that is constantly being made and remade, humans continue to design (and be re-designed by) the one thing that makes them different from other species: the human brain. After 400 years of thinking of the brain as a machine, we now know that thought can change both the structure and function of our brains — the ephemeral can change matter. The plasticity of the brain, Norman Doidge (2007) points out, makes it highly resilient, but a resilient brain is more vulnerable to the influences of new technologies (especially because they are so pervasive). The cellphone and the tablet have become for many an extension of the physical self by their proximity and availability; these technologies are specifically designed to attract and hold our attention (Wu 2016).

Disruptive forces

For teachers, new media can act as disruptive forces. Media may provide a competitor for student attention and interest, as well as providing access to ongoing communication with peers. Depending on how teachers plan for instruction, digital technologies, with their multimodal, multimedia, and communication capacities, may be embraced, or, as happens in some schools, devices may be locked away. Teachers and often school administrators are obliged to make complex decisions, based on a constantly shifting technology and mediascape (Appadurai 1990).

A constant urge to shift and change

The constant shift and change — which is what attracts our attention — creates a need for shift and change; our mammalian brain — the "old" one that lies just at the top of the brain stem — has always been on the alert for that "next thing." Today lulls, silences, moments when nothing is happening are regarded as "boring" and to be avoided. We think of the plays of Harold Pinter and Samuel Beckett and their rich catalogue of words to describe such quiet moments: "silence," "pause," "breath," "wait," "breathes" — they surely would create a digital hell for some people today! But it is in the moments of "nothing happening" that we can think, imagine, and dream (Turkle 2015, 62–63).

A loss of empathy

The distance that devices create results in a tendency to be less careful about how we connect to each other. The opportunities for anonymity can create a disdain for others' feelings, undermining civility. In their analysis of the impact of digital devices, Konrath and her colleagues (2011) report that among college students, empathy had dropped by 40 percent. That is the digital reality: we are losing face-to-face connections in a three-dimensional world in exchange for a virtual two-dimensional reality that takes place through and behind a screen.

Texting conversations completely ignore what happens in the immediacy of an actual conversation: the subtle shifts of face and body as we respond to each other's words and the practices of thinking aloud, hearing the words and rethinking them, rephrasing and shifting tone and emphasis in order to achieve clarity. To join in such a conversation is to imagine another mind, to empathize and to enjoy gesture, and to share humor and irony through the medium of talk (Turkle 2015, 105).

Effective Questioning as a Response

What we have presented so far calls for action. We do not pretend to have the answers, but we do suggest that revisiting questioning in classrooms is needed more than ever: the range of ways we and our students can seek answers is quickly expanding, as is the democratic access to publication. An effective question attracts attention, stimulates interest by generating that earliest of capacities, curiosity, and, in a rich context of support, enables focused attention. In our roles as parents, teachers, counsellors, mentors, and friends, we need to ask the sorts of questions that encourage the following capacities:

* critical thinking, also known as "thoughtful reasoning"
* empathic awareness: the ability to feel things *as if we were the other*
* a reflective stance: the ability to analyze, appraise, and assess to consider personal experiences, beliefs, and assumptions *in relation to others'* points of view

In Chapter 3, we consider each of these capacities individually, recognizing that any effort to separate them would be like separating the skillfully spun threads of a swath of fine wool which holds echoes of each in the other.

Chapter 3 Three Capacities to Enlarge the Conversation

Students today manage massive amounts of information and data, and they can often do this better and more efficiently than their teachers. However, the issue for teaching and learning is not so much about managing as it is about how to process, question, reflect on, and make meaning out of the material. Under "Effective Questioning as a Response," in Chapter 2, we suggested that questioning enabled three capacities that are significant players in counteracting the negative effects of digital media: (1) critical thinking, (2) empathic awareness, and (3) a reflective stance. While critical thinking and reflection are often integral to each other, empathic awareness allows us to add our personal experiences and perspectives to mediate and deepen understanding.

Critical Thinking

Students in elementary and high schools can engage in projects that enhance school and community awareness about issues, such as recycling programs (see Chapter 11). When they do so, they will begin to demonstrate a sense of agency.

To think critically, we need to be able to ask powerful questions. These questions should provide information, have the possibility of connecting in some way with each participant, be open, be unexpected or surprising perhaps, and elicit answers that may not come quickly, if ever (Case 2005; Petress 2004). Critical thinking enables us to examine the deep structures that create the surface content. The latter might raise a question like this: "How can we change and address the conditions of poverty?" Critical thinking would go deeper, prompting us to consider "What makes and keeps people impoverished?" Such considerations can empower people to struggle against forces that constrain them from speaking back to power.

For Richard Paul and Linda Elder (2001), a critical thinker is a person who "improves the quality of his or her thinking" by remaining open-minded. Such a thinker recognizes and assesses assumptions and forecasts implications. James Zull (2002) suggests that while passive students receive, remember, and integrate information, engaged learners involved with critical thinking go deeper to discover how to act, modify, create, control, and test out information.

Critical thinking is a process rather than an end (Scriven and Paul 2003). Asking questions and proffering possible answers requires of participants a mutual awareness, a healthy skepticism, and a willingness to examine their own beliefs, assumptions, and opinions (Ferrett 1997). This kind of thinking also has a creative component. As we build abstract thought through use of our imaginations, we make new connections between ideas and reshape our thinking in ways that reveal new possibilities (Petress 2004).

Critical thinking is about raising the kinds of questions generated by living richly in the present. It is having both the ability and interest to look closely and deeply at what is happening, what is said, what is left unsaid, and what is the emotional climate. Individuals respond in terms of their political, social, cultural, ethical, and personal perspectives, including an awareness of how their own questions and concerns shape, reflect, contradict, and inform the group. In turn, their perceptions will be shaped by the group's responses. It is important to remember that some (or many) people may disagree as groups come together for a variety of underlying reasons. As Preston (2016) tells us, just "[b]ecause people may appear to do activities together, it does not mean that they share common values, either with each other, or with the social structures within which the activities occur" (19).

Building a healthy community of inquiry

"What characterizes the psyche of a generation that grows up never knowing a world without lone-wolf terrorist attacks? What's the effect of seeing those just ahead of you stumble financially, burdened by university debt? What does it mean that your life — your brand — plays out on Instagram and Facebook and Twitter, with the expectation and responsibility of being both the watched and the watcher?"
— Erin Anderssen (2016, F3)

Human beings are quite good at navigating such seemingly complex relationships. According to Jonothan Neelands's (1984) idea of "conspectus," a healthy community of inquiry is a community that invites every idea and accepts that all ideas have value and purpose. Rather than assuming consensus we can use difference to explore even more deeply. Central to critical pedagogy is the ability to see the world from many points of view, to be comfortable shifting back and forth as we change perspectives, challenge stereotypes, explore alternatives, and question motives.

When we ask the kinds of questions that require students to think deeply and grapple with ideas that matter, they begin to interrogate, or examine, their own learning. They make connections among, between, and beyond themselves; they encounter ideas and dilemmas that demand empathic attention (Saxton and Miller 2015). "Better questions enable us to name what we see around us — the hunger, the passivity, the homelessness, the 'silences' . . . [It] requires imagination to be conscious of them [the things around us], to find our own lived worlds lacking because of them," writes Maxine Greene (1995, 111). These conversations offer ways of exploring the big questions about what it means to be human and alive in the world — and doing so is an integral component of empathy.

Empathic Awareness

To be aware empathically, we need the ability to understand what another is thinking, "to ascribe beliefs, desires, fears and hope to someone else" (Dunbar 1996). That, however, is only the cognitive component of empathy, known as "Theory of Mind" (Premack and Woodruff 1978). For this cognitive component, Goldstein, Wu, and Winner (2009) use the example of bullies who know how to upset others and understand the effects of their behavior but don't care.

There is also another element we need to consider: one that serves to *deepen* that cognitive understanding, that is, *feeling as the other feels*, or experiencing directly another's emotional state. Martin Buber (1965)

"Deep listening is to see oneself in a caring partnership with others. It is generous, non-judgmental, contemplative and open to others' thoughts and feelings."
— CMind (2015)

describes this emotional engagement best as "glid[ing] with one's own feeling into the dynamic structure of [another] . . . to trace it from within . . . with the perceptions of one's own muscles" (97). This is a deeper feeling of connection — a whole-body response that attunes to others and is indicative of *deep listening*, an essential skill for collaboration and community.

Thinking and talking as members of a community rather than as individuals has the potential for the development of group emotion, and we likely know the shared joy that results from feeling we are all connected (see Berg and Seeber 2016).

Using role to explore perspectives

As drama teachers, we, the authors, are aware of the benefits of how embodiment, or the taking on of roles, can enrich those discussions empathically. Assuming a role enables us to see more clearly from alternative views within the safety that the role provides. Of course, we all take on many roles every day — teacher, parent, daughter or son, academic, and more. Roles are not exclusive to the actor. We can use our capacity for perspective taking as part of our pedagogy. Questioning in role enables the respondent to see a possible situation from a personal perspective, as well as a theoretical one. For example:

Discipline: *Environmental Science*
Question in role: *As a climate change denier, how might you frame your concerns at a meeting of flood victims?*

Discipline: *Robotics*
Question in role: *As a robot involved in research for the development of next-stage robotics, what concerns do you have for your future?*

The use of role in teaching offers many possibilities for enlarging the conversation through empathic awareness and the deepening of critical thinking. It adds the immediacy of a personal investment.

Key to the development of learning, whether it be critical thinking or empathic awareness, is reflection. And at the heart of the reflective process is the space it provides to bring into being a personal relationship with the content and concepts of the material under study.

Reflection

Reflection is the means by which we create meaning from our experiences; without offering students and participants the opportunity to reflect, we seriously limit the effects of personal learning. "Reflection," writes Jenny Moon (2004), "lies somewhere around the notion of learning and thinking. We reflect in order to learn something, or we learn as a result of reflecting" (n.p.). Transforming experience through reflection into long-term memory is how we build our life stories.

James Zull (2002) reminds us that feelings are integral to our capacity for reflection. The kinds of reflective questions we ask should enable learners to "put things together" cognitively and emotionally to build patterns that can be mentally referenced for future meaning and decision making (Barrett 2005; Damasio 2000). Reflection allows time to consider the attitudes, principles, and beliefs that lie beneath the material; it permits us to see these in relation to the views, actions, and feelings of others. It lets us see how ideas are mediated and how thought is changed when it becomes public.

Reflection may be both an individual and a group activity. Through reflection, participants have an opportunity to consider bigger issues and questions, and to set those considerations within the wider context of their cultures. As the first simple thoughts in conversation bounce back and forth, they become more complex, raising, as Daniel Siegel (2007) notes, "the awareness of being aware." And this thinking about thinking (metacognition) is how we learn as we are reorganizing our long-term memory, "providing additional cues that can be used to retrieve specific memories" (252).

Reflecting is not only about trying to fit experience into memory but also about how to think about the meanings we are making. Whether an individual agrees with others' points of view and expressed feelings or not, it is important to hear those points of view and emotional responses. It is through the healthy promotion of *conspectus* (Neelands 1984) that "the right to be understood is [discovered to be] more important than owning the truth" (Kundera 1986/1988, 169). Katzenbach and Smith report, "Conflicting views and experiences [come to be seen] as a source of strength" (1993, 128).

Eric Booth (1999) notes how hard it is for people to reflect. "Many have an ingrained bias against such an activity deeming their thoughts not worth noticing but once begun they come to respect experience-awareness as a skill that directly taps into the feeling of being alive" (54). We have noted the same response through the years: a definite reluctance in students to engage in what they regard as a kind of speculative fiction. They are used to dealing with facts and with familiarity.

Identifying key questions

One way we have found to encourage student ownership and fuller engagement is to identify for ourselves the **key questions or understandings** at the heart of what is being taught (the content). These provide the direction and reference points for reflection, whether that takes place during the lesson, as part of the conclusion, or as a link back to the content to prepare for what is to come. Key questions act as the container for deeper and more universal understanding about things that matter. They offer possible themes and opportunities to enable reflection that moves from the particulars of the content to the universal issues that the content addresses. For example, in a lesson about dictatorship, the following provided the direction for exploring issues of tyranny:

- There are many ways to use power for control.
- How is it that dictatorships are able to thrive?
- What drives the decision to take a stand? (Miller and Saxton 2016, 91)

Reflection offers the time and the opportunity to examine, to think about, and to become conscious of the ways in which we reacted, the words we spoke, the ideas we formed, and the feelings we expressed.

Reflection Prompts

- Talk to the person next to you about that . . . (experience, activity, discussion).
- What did you hear from your partner?
- How might you describe what we have done today to someone who was away?

Examples of Key Questions and Understandings for Younger Students

What importance do memories play in our lives?
What is it about intergenerational relationships that hold special meaning?
Stories play an important role in our lives.
(Miller and Saxton 2016)

I Wonder . . .

If the world is progressing, I wonder what it is that is getting better and what we might consider as steps backward?

"Quizzes, examinations, and aptitude tests all reinforce the value of correct answers. Is it any wonder that most of us are uncomfortable with not knowing?"
— Eric E. Vogt, Juanita Brown, and David Isaacs (2003, 2)

As Linda Laidlaw (2005, 144) puts it, in these reflective conversations, "intricate details, complex interconnections and interrelations, the layering of experiences, events, histories and memories . . ." "dance together in . . . 'orderly disorder'" (Doll 2008). Reflection is, paradoxically, not just a way of looking back but a means of imagining a future and expanding our worldview.

Through questioning critically, empathically, and reflectively, participants may begin to find in themselves a sense of agency, something they need as they navigate the shifting sands of their experiences. Nevertheless, implicit learning — often represented by fixed ideas and unquestioned cultural views that sink into our lives as we develop and mature — can be very resistant to change. When our minds lock onto something, it is stored in a direct way, creating nodes of neural firing patterns that form the building blocks of our world knowledge. "The primacy of answers *as assurances of competence* is present in many aspects of our lives . . . as well as in our classrooms," states Berger (2014, 139). It is not, however, too useful for the young people with whom we work. Nor is it helpful for grappling with matters in our diverse and unsettled world.

Up to this point, we have examined the current context in which many of us are working. We have noted how that is affected by the rewards and challenges of technology, and we have considered our affective capacities for mediating the onslaught of information through digital media. In Chapter 4, we offer an example unit that highlights the three capacities we have described and how they can be seen in action.

Chapter 4   Leaving Home: Using the Questioning Capacities

This unit is based on the experiences of authors Linda Laidlaw and Joanne O'Mara working with students aged 11 to 18 in Canada and Australia. It reflects their collaboration and the breadth of resources they were able to share.

We have selected the topic "Leaving Home" to provide examples of how the three questioning capacities — critical thinking, empathic awareness, and reflection — might be represented in questioning and inquiry. Students in diverse classrooms may share many different personal connections to key understandings that underlie the many themes represented. As Canadian children's literature scholar Lynne Wiltse (2015) suggests, literature and source materials can provide both "mirrors" whereby students can see their own experiences reflected back and "windows" that can open views on the world beyond one's self, shifting understanding.

Integrating Curriculum

A range of content areas with a connection to this topic can be found across curricula: immigration, refugees, the history of Indian Residential Schools in Canada and elsewhere, and other intersecting areas of inquiry in Social Studies. Leaving Home also lends itself to numerous literature studies in English Language Arts classes, from picture books to young adult novels. Furthermore, students in environmental science may investigate global migration patterns, environmental responses to climate change, and the difficulties and displacements that climate change causes for flora, fauna, and species that live in water. A wealth of excellent sources address these and related themes, often including links to social justice issues, some of which are listed at the end of the chapter.

In our example process, we address the three capacities and ways in which teachers might offer students opportunities to invest themselves in the material and help to guide the course of classroom exploration. Our strategies address questioning and inquiry aimed at upper elementary to middle secondary grades, but these may be adapted for use with younger students or at the upper secondary level. For ease of reading, we have developed a chronological flow, but the components of this inquiry may be used independently and applied to other inquiry topics.

Ways to approach questioning

As noted in Chapter 1, questioning is a democratic skill all citizens need to develop. Good questioning in teaching and learning can support students in making powerful connections to others (empathic awareness); examining critically the world around them, texts, and content; and developing deeper reflection skills to strengthen learning. Teachers and students can bring together and "remix" information and different forms of representation and text (Pahl and Rowsell 2012), using a range of modalities, including print, oral discussion, media images, and digital audio and video recordings, as a part of their investigations. Here, we use image as a "way in" to questioning and eliciting students' own wonderings.

Part 1: Working from Image — The Life Jacket

You can find the image of Ben Quilty's *High Tide Mark* at https://www.ngv.vic.gov.au/explore/collection/work/122147/.

In this lesson, we refer to a Ben Quilty painting of a life jacket from an Australian collection. The image is available online. Alternatively, you may want to begin the lesson with an actual life jacket, placed on the floor.

We offer the following as a series of strategies in an inquiry process, providing possible related teacher talk.

1. Attracting attention and gaining interest

Focus: To tap into students' personal experiences of receiving help

> Teacher (*asking the whole class*): When, I wonder, have you had an experience where you had someone or something to help you?

> *Students share their responses.*

> Teacher: You have likely heard the expression "They threw me a life jacket," and for some of your experiences, that metaphor will be very appropriate. Today, we are going to explore that idea through an image.

2. Introducing the painting

Focus: To record first impressions (critical viewing)

The teacher shares Ben Quilty's painting, *High Tide Mark*, projecting the image onto a digital screen, if possible. This artwork presents a powerful image of a vivid orange life jacket set on a dark background. Students study the image and offer words of description and interpretation. The teacher helps students explore the painting.

Teacher prompts:

- What do you notice about this painting?
- What is it about the painting that draws us in?
- What do you think this painting might represent?
- I wonder why someone would choose to paint such an object?
- If you think as an artist, what kind of story can you imagine as you look at this painting?

3. Discovering the story behind the painting

Focus: Seeing from the artist's perspective

> Teacher: Now that we've begun to explore this painting, listen as I read the description from the Gallery catalogue:

The impasto-style painting *High tide mark*, 2016, was the result of the artist travelling that year to Greece, Serbia and Lebanon to witness firsthand the global refugee crisis. On a beach in Lesbos, Quilty observed a 'high tide mark' of bright orange life jackets, discarded by Syrian asylum seekers as they reached the shore after making the perilous journey across open ocean from Turkey. In Quilty's words, the vest symbolises the 'ocean of humans that have moved across those waters', themselves dislocated and dispersed like the cast-off jackets.

Students listen to the text from the National Gallery of Victoria, Melbourne.

4. What can we learn from this painting?

Focus: To bring initial interpretations into a relationship with the artist's interpretation (building empathic awareness)

Teacher: Knowing the background to this painting, what do you imagine could be the story of this life jacket and the person or persons who have worn it?

In pairs or small groups, students reflect on the image. They consider how knowing the story of the painting has possibly changed their interpretations. They record key ideas from their conversation. They may make notes or short audio recordings.

[Later on, students can use these notes as a part of their inquiries and as research texts.]

5. What questions do we have?

Focus: To arrive at the questions to which they want to find the answers

The teacher gathers the class together to generate questions and activate reflection.

Teacher prompts:

- What questions are beginning to form in your mind?
- What do you wonder about?
- What questions will help you imagine the life of the person who might have worn this vest and cast it off?

As students share their questions, the teacher records them.

6. Finding answers

Focus: To see questions as tools for discovery

The teacher poses these questions to help prepare students for research.

Teacher prompts:

- How might we go about finding answers to these questions?
- What sources could we investigate to help us learn more?
- What kinds of texts might we use to find reliable information?
- What tells us that this information is reliable?
- Who might we ask for additional information?

There are many options for students to "dig deeper" through independent or collaborative research activities to follow up on their questions. Depending on the class's responses and questions, students might engage in a range of different inquiries, such as examining and comparing online resources, exploring print and text resources, meeting with librarians (from either school or community libraries), writing letters to the artist, and interviewing refugee organization personnel. Reflective writing and articulating further thoughts and wonderings about the Ben Quilty painting provide two more possibilities.

The teacher may recognize that some of the questions raised in this inquiry remain difficult to answer, despite student research efforts. These kinds of questions may be better explored through fictional inquiries, where deeper empathic understanding can be nurtured through imaginative writing or work in role. For example, a student could take on the perspective of the person who used this life vest and be interviewed by another student as journalist; tell the story of the journey by composing a letter to send to those family members left behind; or take the role of a grandparent relating memories of the experience on an anniversary of becoming a citizen of the new country.

We follow up these initial steps by making a link to a fictional literature source with a focus on immigration and refugees.

Part 2: Asking Questions in Response to Literature — Shaun Tan's *The Arrival*

Many excellent picture books, graphic novels, and novels present perspectives relating to leaving home stories — often representing what Louise Rosenblatt (1978/1988) labels "efferent texts." Such texts provide information that, in addition to the pleasure of the reading experience, might be used for further purposes after the reading event. Questions are key for literature study to assist students in developing critical thinking and supporting processes of resymbolization. They thereby help enable students to make meaning of texts.

We have chosen *The Arrival*, a wordless picture book by Shaun Tan which tells stories of immigrant experiences. This graphic novel offers complex and sophisticated illustrations that must be "read" and interpreted and leaves many interpretive gaps (Miller and Saxton 2004, 2016). It thus presents numerous openings for asking good questions.

1. Playing a familiar game

Focus: To engage with the theme

The teacher invites students to play "I'm packing my backpack to visit my grandma [or uncle, or whatever] and in it I put . . ." In this cumulative packing game students recount what has been offered and add what they would take on their trip. The game elicits a great deal of laughter and often mention of some strange and interesting items.

Resymbolization is the finding of new meanings and new forms of expression as one becomes more familiar with the object or text of interest.

A Way In by Video

An excellent animated adaptation of *The Arrival*, created by Frederik Vorndran, blends the illustrations of the text with a powerful soundtrack. An alternative to sharing the initial pages of the book is to share the first 45 seconds of the video. Students might then be invited to examine the use of music and sound effects for their contributions to interpretation and meaning making. See https://vimeo.com/74292820.

Furthermore, numerous video or book reviews exist. Of particular note is a series of interviews with Shaun Tan on YouTube, where the author/illustrator shares his sketchbook and perspectives on multiculturalism and immigration: https://www.youtube.com/watch?v=Hrs69XiC9fs.

2. Reading a set of pictures

Focus: To build a context for the work

The teacher projects the second page of illustrations from *The Arrival*, Part I: hands wrapping a family photograph — father, mother, and young daughter — and placing the photograph in a suitcase.

> Teacher: Many of us have had the experience of packing a suitcase or a backpack either for a weekend getaway or a long journey. These images capture such a moment. What's your sense of these pictures? (*Students offer their ideas.*)

3. Reading a picture

Focus: To introduce the theme of leaving

The teacher projects the third image: a man and woman holding hands and touching a suitcase.

> Teacher: As you look at this illustration, imagine the thoughts, feelings, and questions shared between the man and the woman. (*Students do so.*)
> I wonder if we can hear some of those thoughts and questions so that we can build a collective interpretation of this drawing. Be sure to share your voice. Speak aloud when there is a space for your thoughts and questions . . .

The words of the participants echo around the room.

4. Exploring the big questions that underlie the theme

Focus: To imagine what it is to leave home

The teacher invites students to relate the theme to their own lives.

> Teacher: You've touched on some important ideas and questions that are part of making a change in our lives, in this case, leaving home. What is it to leave? What do we leave behind? Do we leave behind parts of our identities when we move away? When in your life might you have experienced something like this? Turn to the person next to you and listen to each other's story . . . (*Students learn from their partners' experiences.*)
> What connections can you make to the illustrations we have been looking at?

The teacher takes time for some students to share.

5. Reprise of the packing game

Focus: Reflecting on what we are learning through play

The teacher directs the students to play a new version of the packing game.

> Teacher: Having shared some of our stories, let's play that packing game again. This time let's respond to "I am leaving my home and I can't leave without my . . ."

Students' responses will be more serious. For example, the teacher might hear, "My cellphone because then I would have all my photos and contacts" or "My special necklace that my mother gave me."

> Teacher: What might be the sorts of situations where people would need to pack up and leave home?

Students may make links to their own histories, moves from former homes, family migration stories, and situations they know about. Many students in one class knew students who had evacuated from the Alberta Fort McMurray fire in 2016. Other students knew of families in their community who had come to their city as recent refugees; others talked about a child in foster care.

The use of literature to gain critical tools

In our literature example, we have used questions that aim to go below the surface of the story and bring together the three capacities. By so doing, we can help students to gain empathy for and understanding of people who leave their homes for a new life elsewhere. We can also encourage students to reflect on personal connections as well as those that may be less familiar to them.

Through work with literature, students may further their critical thinking. They can gain new critical tools "for weighing and critiquing, analysing and appraising textual techniques and ideologies, values and positions" (Luke, O'Brien, and Comber 1994, 139). These tools are especially important following the emergence of "fake news" as a political tool. Critical literacy requires taking a dialogic approach to education (Freire 1974), an opening up of conversations and questions that support such discussions. Part 3 promotes this further.

Part 3: Developing a Research and Response Text

Part 3 moves into more independent student inquiry and questioning. We borrow from an interpretive research strategy developed by Dennis Sumara (1998) and used in a literature study. Students were asked to read and respond to a text in multiple modes and forms. In our adaptation, students considered topics they wanted to explore more deeply in connection to their own interests and earlier Leaving Home activities, researching their topics and creating essays or short texts that brought together their ideas from these literacy experiences.

However, a powerful method of bringing together student research from multiple sources — their own experiences, readings, viewings, online and library research — is to have students create a screencast, a short video presentation where they incorporate several modes of representation: written text, visual images, and an audio track.

There are many different structures and applications that might be taken up to create a screencast. Slideshow programs such as PowerPoint, Keynote, or Google Slides (or whichever presentation software is currently in use in the classroom) can be used to create the basic "canvas," with audio voice-over added in as a second step. Finally, screen-recording

For additional resources, see http://teachingkidsnews.com.

software, such as Screencast-o-Matic or QuickTime Player, can be used to capture the final presentation. Alternatively, students might make a movie trailer to capture their ideas and create the screencast, using a movie-making application. The final pieces can be shared in the classroom or uploaded online to share with students' families.

Both types of projects — screencasts and essays — include factual research, student connections to the literature source, image viewing, and student representations of their reflections, interpretations, and thinking. The teacher's role in projects of either kind is essential. It is not enough to send students to the library — or online — and expect a good result. Asking students to consider their sources will help them to develop their critical thinking skills further. Providing information about bias and point of view is also important. Finally, such work should involve students in critically reviewing, examining, and reflecting on their completed writing and video texts.

Teacher prompts:
• How might we know which sorts of texts or media sources are accurate?
• How can we identify what might be "fake news" sources?
• What have you learned from your responses and research?
• When you consider the theme of leaving home, what do you think about now?
• What have you learned from your classmates' writing or screencasts that you didn't know before?
• In what ways might we move from our questions and research to other sorts of actions?

Research from a Safe Distance

While the Leaving Home topic can be difficult, its themes and issues are important and are typically at the centre of social studies curricula. Using objects or images as the centre of an inquiry provides a focus for the students and enables a virtual world to be built around them as they become invested with symbolic meanings. Enacting different roles (e.g., through dramatic representation, playing out a character in a digital game, reading or writing about a situation through the eyes of a character) enables the development of empathic responses. At the same time, the activities described make it possible for students to look at what otherwise might be a situation too challenging or emotionally charged. Positioning their research at a "slight remove" makes it possible for students to do research at their own comfort levels. Shaun Tan puts this well in an online discussion about the creation of *The Arrival:*

> One of the great powers of storytelling is that it invites us to walk in other people's shoes for a while, but perhaps even more importantly, it invites us to contemplate our own shoes also. We might do well to think of ourselves as possible strangers in our own strange land. What conclusions we draw from this are unlikely to be easily summarised, all the more reason to think further on the connections between people and places, and what we might mean when we talk about "belonging." (Tan: Accessed 2018)

Leaving Home Resources to Increase Empathy

GAMES

Digital games can be very effective in helping young people to imagine experiences. High-quality games are based on reliable information and set up a factually based virtual world. Many "serious" games about asylum seekers can be found online. A few are outlined here.

- **Could You Survive?** The United Nations High Commissioner for Refugees (UNHCR) has developed digital games (apps available for Android and Apple devices) to enable others to experience some of the complexity of the everyday questions and decisions that asylum seekers ask and make. The game Could You Survive? is designed to help players increase their empathy. It asks, "If conflict threatened your family, what would you do?" This game is suitable for junior-high students and, as an extension activity, students could play through a story.

  There are three different scenarios that follow the stories of different characters. The scenarios ask, "Can you imagine being so desperate to escape that you pay a smuggler to help you? Can you imagine the terror of being caught by the army you were fleeing from? Can you imagine the trauma of being separated from your family by war?" The game can be found at https://mylifeasarefugee.org/game.html.

- *Syrian Journey* — **An Interactive Escape Story:** The BBC story *Syrian Journey: Choose Your Own Escape Route* is another excellent online resource: see http://www.bbc.com/news/world-middle-east-32057601.

  In this interactive digital story, readers choose who they are and what they will do along the journey, then find out what might happen. In class, upper elementary to upper secondary students might work through these scenarios in small groups and then discuss what they discovered and share how their characters fared. After playing the game, students could develop narrative, expository, or critical compositions or do other writing tasks.

BOOKS AND OTHER RESOURCES BY THEME

Refugees:
- *The Boat* is an interactive digital graphic novel adaptation by Matt Huynh of a story by Nam Le (https://www.sbs.com.au/theboat/). This resource also includes classroom resources.
  Level: High school (sophisticated content)

How might these questions be opened to invite discussion rather than the possibility of short answers, such as "yes," "no," or "I don't know"?

- *My Beautiful Birds* by Suzanne Del Rizzo is based on a true story of Syrian refugees.
  Level: Elementary
- *Out* by Angela May George and Owen Swan concerns a girl and her mother fleeing their homeland in search of asylum.
  Levels: Elementary and junior high

Colonization:
- *The Rabbits*, written by John Marsden and illustrated by Shaun Tan, presents an allegorical tale of an invasion. Rabbits take over the homeland of the people who were there before them.
  Levels: Elementary and secondary

Indian Residential Schools:
- *Fatty Legs: A True Story* is written by Christy Jordan-Fenton and Margaret Pokiak-Fenton. It tells what life was like for an eight-year-old Indigenous girl forced to leave her family and attend an Indian Residential School in Canada.
  Levels: Grades 5 to 8
- *When I Was Eight*, also by Christy Jordan-Fenton and Margaret Pokiak-Fenton, tells the same story as *Fatty Legs* in easier language and with illustrations. (It can be found on YouTube: https://www.youtube.com/watch?v=LSBrkJn3NeI.)
  Level: Elementary
- *When We Were Alone*, written by David A. Robertson and illustrated by Julie Flett, features a grandmother telling her granddaughter about life at an Indian Residential School where she was at great risk of losing her Indigenous culture. It won a Governor General's Literary Award in 2017.
  Level: Primary
- *Secret Path* is a graphic novel by Gord Downie and Jeff Lemire, with a 10-song digital download album by Downie. It is also a film. *Secret Path* tells the true story of a 12-year-old Ojibwa boy who runs away from the Indian Residential School where he has been placed to try to get home. He dies of exposure.
  Level: High school (sophisticated content)

Chapter 5   Shifting Language to Reflect a Shifting World

One day when doing research that involved the idea of balance, Juliana and Carole talked with Bill Doll, the curriculum theorist.

"Tell us," we asked, "about how to achieve balance."

"I don't think," he said tactfully as he folded himself into an armchair, "that, in most things, balance is something you always want to achieve. Yes, if you are walking the high wire and trying to balance a cup of tea and a plate of cookies."

But for a human being to be balanced, he pointed out, it is to be in *stasis* and stasis is not a growing state; it is, rather, a state of stability, inactivity, stagnation — impervious to change and development.

"It is more preferable to teeter," he went on, "because in movement, there is always possibility" (Doll 2011, in conversation).

For Bill Doll and for many current educational thinkers, the nature of balance can be equated with the comforts of certainty in which someone else provides the answers and we are not called upon to make "hard calls" or tough judgments.

The False Positive of Certainty

We have a need for certainty, for closure — we like to know answers. We remember ourselves as children demanding to go to the park, the lake, wherever, and being in an agony of frustration when our parents answered, "it depends" or "we'll see." In adults that need to know is heightened when we are short of time and stressed or, equally, bored or tired. Yet much certainty is like a "false positive" in that, while we may want it, it is not good for us. Certainty provides the answers about which we do not need to think; it closes the door of possibilities. In this chapter, we look at how the language we use in questioning can cause the kind of "teetering" that encourages the exploration of possibilities.

Something happens in our brains when we gather and process what is on offer. Depending on how we are taught, our brain uses different filing systems which Daniel Kahneman (2011) names "Fast" and "Slow." Instructional language is indicative, factual, general, and *fast*. Nicola Perullo (2007) calls it "supermarket thought" — standardized and easily reproducible. It tells you what to do, is based on what you have learned and — it is implied — is applicable in all circumstances, suppressing doubt and building coherence (114). Instructional, or "absolute," language is, of course, a remarkably efficient way of transmitting knowledge, channelling the thinking down clearly indicated paths with defined outcomes. The response to instructional language is rote or memory based and can be accessed easily and quickly (if you were paying attention) from the "drawer" into which it has been filed. Instructional language is the means through which most of us in the teaching profession were taught.

Based on our recent experience in educational institutions, we can say that "fast" is still pretty much the system of choice. And one can see why. The traditional view is that someone is in charge of learning. That person holds the knowledge and the rest of us are there to soak it in. The relationship is comfortable, and yet the world *has* changed, and we now recognize that change is a condition of existence.

A future always in motion

What has happened, what is happening, and what will happen is always *contingent*, that is to say, "dependent upon something that is not yet certain" (Stein 1966, 316). And that reality — chaotic, complex, provisional — must *surely* be reflected in how we prepare our students to deal with the world's uncertainties, ambiguities, and complexities. Only when our language reflects the conditionality of the world will students gain the tools to work with that sense of impermanence and become more comfortable, creative, and flexible in how they use what they are learning.

We propose that teaching instructions, information, prompts, problems, responses, questions, challenges, and reflections sometimes be offered in *conditional* rather than in instructional language. Only with this modelling will students see the language of their school world match the fluidity of their shifting experiences.

What Is Conditional Language?

Conditional words, such as *might, could be, might entail, may on occasion, could involve, may have,* and *could have been,* create a quite different response in the brain than the absolutes *is, are,* and *were.* They awaken the brain to engage more fully with the whole mind. When we teach conditionally, couching the material in words and phrases not cut and dried, the information passes through many more and different neural networks than it does with the use of absolutes. This "slow" thinking is capable of doubt because "it can maintain incompatible possibilities at the same time" — for example, on the one hand and on the other (Kahneman 2011, 114).

Conditional statements are tentative, so the patterns of neural networks must be more intricately connected if they are to be included as knowledge. We need to link the "may" and the "at times" conditions to *all* the moments of possibility in which a given point may or may not apply. Because the brain is working hard, the mind is vigorously engaged. We are better able to view a situation from several perspectives; we are drawn not only to the information but also to the *context* in which it is set. Because of the novelty, we create new categories through which information may be understood. With learning offered as conditional, we

VUCA

This 1990s military acronym reflected an emerging recognition that the world was no longer predictable. It was later picked up by the business community, but the four words below still create a sense of unease in educational contexts:
V = Volatility
U = Uncertainty
C = Complexity
A = Ambiguity
— Judith Stiehm and Nicholas Townsend (2002, 6)

"Conditional statements offered in direct oral or written material seem to induce a cognitively mindful state that evokes the active engagement of the student's own mind."
— Daniel Siegel (2007, 232)

Direct versus Conditional Question

Direct: What makes a community?
Conditional: What might be some of the elements that make up a community?

are required to keep an open mind, attentive to the possibility of the new and in a "state of healthy uncertainty" (Siegel 2007, 232–33).

Of course, the indicative voice is important and useful; we are not suggesting that it be abandoned. It is, after all, a quick way to get to the place where thought and reflection may *then* take their time. When an earthquake struck Christchurch, New Zealand, on February 22, 2011, we did not need to hear our host teacher ask if it might be possible for us to consider moving towards the door. He simply said, "Door, now!" We were grateful for his decisive and informed instruction!

The Potential of the Conditional

You will meet students who are not used to a conditional mode of teaching and are discomfited by the demands it makes of them: to think, to reflect, to relate, to struggle to make it their own. As with all new ideas, it takes time for students to embrace the challenges this new way of thinking demands. Ellen Langer (1997) and others (Powers 2011; Ritchart and Perkins 2000) have been researching uses of conditional language since the 1990s. Their findings suggest that those who are taught conditionally, be they athletes or medical, dance, mathematics, or physics students, have a greater ability for recall, are more aware of the importance of contexts, and take a more flexible approach in context-driven situations. Beyond that, they enjoy their work more because the brain is working harder.

Perhaps, though, you are already a vigorous user of the conditional.

Philosopher Richard Sennett (2012) remembers coming from his studies at New York's Juilliard School to rehearse with English instrumentalists in London. He was surprised at their use of the conditional, discovering that *possibly*, *perhaps*, and *I would have thought* opened spaces for experiment; such tentativeness "offered an invitation to others to join in" (22). The "indeterminate mutual space" created by use of the conditional is one, he writes, "where strangers can dwell with one another and where discussions can take an unforeseen direction" (23).

Interestingly, Sennett notes that the conditional is the tense most used in diplomacy. He points out that it engenders the attendant skills of deep listening and the abilities to use and read silences, manage disagreements, and avoid frustration — all necessary to the taking in of others' points of view. Here is conversation at its most enriched and enriching — creative dialogues that include all speakers in range, aware that we are not "speaking about" but rather, "to and with others, keeping the discourse open-ended: critiquing, interrupting, empowering and questioning" (Denzin 1997, 121).

Conditional language is not only a way to open thought, feeling, and talk; it is also a gentle and respectful way to open ourselves and others to the possible, and to let disagreements, resistance, and conflicts become appreciated for what they can add to the talk or discussion. The very uncertainties that conditional language sets in play may, with time, become a means of interrupting our worldviews, reframing our relationships, and enabling us to rethink our preconceptions (Weigler 2015, 8–11).

For some of us, living is an exciting, demanding, and infinitely engaging state; its challenges, issues, troubles, joys, and fulfillments are life enhancing. For others, mere surviving demands resilience and a sense of self that can withstand the mental, physical, and spiritual assaults that threaten. For all of us, there are capacities that make us human: imagination, creativity, the ability to see something from many different points of view, working not only as an individual but with others, making friends, being intimate and loving, playing, caring, and *finding out*. These capacities lie within each of us, and they are what we are in danger of losing as we become more pressured, less reflective, and less practised in human interaction.

The Need to Cultivate Emotional and Intellectual Resilience

Previous chapters have introduced several ideas that, while not new, have gained a greater integrity since the publication of the second edition of *Asking Better Questions*. The deep infiltration of the digital world as a shaper and remaker of the 21st century now requires us to reconsider the power of questioning as a means of developing more thoughtful, empathic, and reflective responses to situations and events.

The old *who*, *what*, *where*, *when*, and *how* engendered hope of answers that would provide closure. We now know that, in today's shifting landscapes, such expectations are much less possible. When we see uncertainty as a powerful force for allowing things to happen, the language of diplomacy may open our minds to the pleasures of moving through a world that remains curious, odd, ambiguous, and fascinating. The ability to hone our ancient and innate capacity for asking questions should help us cultivate emotional and intellectual resilience. We will need this resilience as a safeguard when the answers raise as many questions again.

The better the questions are, the better we will be. No conditional there!

Chapter 6 Anchors in This Shifting World — Two Structures

Questions to Consider When Planning for Oral Discussion

• What kinds of thinking is this question generating?
• How will this question help participants engage in and with the material?

According to Stephen Brookfield (2015), classrooms reflect the confusion of a world that is contingent, changing, and uncertain. Brookfield consequently called classroom teachers "gladiators of ambiguity" working in places that are "bafflingly chaotic" (94). Those of us who may not be teachers but are engaged with the public will also recognize the aptness of his metaphor. All of us will be happy to know that for the gladiators, protective gear is available.

Designed as pedagogical structures of organization, taxonomies can be helpful guides to people looking for direction. A taxonomy is based on orderly classifications, each one dependent upon the one before — cumulatively moving from the simple to the complex. This chapter recommends two taxonomies that may be helpful: one that looks at the different kinds of thinking and one that considers the different ways participants may engage with the materials through questions.

The Evolving Bloom's Taxonomy

The first structure is helpful because it gives us a scaffolding of terms that enable us to plan for or recognize the kinds of thinking at work. *Taxonomy of Educational Objectives: The Classification of Educational Goals* — a.k.a. "Bloom's taxonomy" — provided the last half of the 20th century with a well-documented analysis of the cognitive domain (Bloom 1956; Bloom and Krathwohl 1965). It was not designed as a matrix for questioning, but nevertheless, it became the "go to" reference for teachers planning questions and instruction. Bloom divided thinking into higher and lower levels, and, therefore, teachers naturally assumed that mastery of *lower-*order questions was the prerequisite for *higher-*order questions.

That pattern may be so for *thinking*, but it is not so for *questioning*. Traditionally, educational frames often were viewed as linear and sequential, but as educators we now know that thinking, learning, and questioning are far more complex and recursive. Our research for the first edition of *Asking Better Questions* suggested that any structure that *dictates* the order of a procedure may inhibit natural inquiry. We advised teachers that better questions are contextually responsive, so given that all responses require thought, the answer to a higher-order question will be based upon remembering and understanding.

In 2000, Anderson, Krathwohl, and colleagues revised the cognitive domain taxonomy to encourage a much more open approach to the challenges that learning presents to every individual. Moving the terms from nouns to verbs — as in shifting "Knowledge" to "Remembering" — reflects the activity of thinking more authentically.

Take a moment to compare the original and the revised versions of Bloom's taxonomy.

A Comparison of the Original and Revised Versions of Bloom's Taxonomy

Original 1956/1965	Revised 2002
Lower-Order Thinking Skills	*Lower-Order Thinking Skills*
Knowledge	Remembering
Comprehension	Understanding
Application	Applying
Higher-Order Thinking Skills	*Higher-Order Thinking Skills*
Analysis	Analyzing
Synthesis	Evaluating
Evaluation	Creating

The verb "to create" — to form something out of nothing — was regarded by dictionaries as outside the purview of human-kind until the mid-20th century. (Personal communication, OED editor, 1970)

Now, let's have a look at the revised taxonomy illustrated with questions that explore the life and work of astronaut Chris Hadfield.

Lower-order thinking skills (Revised)

The lower-order thinking skills are identified as (1) remembering, (2) understanding, and (3) applying.

Remembering: Recalling what we already know

> Teacher: In thinking about those who have explored space, what were Chris Hadfield's contributions?

Question stems:
Who . . . ?   Where . . . ?   How . . . ?
What . . . ?   When . . . ?

Understanding: Demonstrating what we know using different patterns of information

> Teacher: How else might we describe him?

Question stems:
What is meant by . . . ?
Can you rephrase . . . ?
Can you describe . . . ?
What is the difference . . . ?
What is the main idea . . . ?

Applying: Applying what we have learned to other situations

> Teacher: What other kinds of people might fit those descriptions?

Question stems:
   Who would you choose?
   What might happen if . . . ?
   How can . . . ?
   What examples . . . ?
   How might you . . . ?

Higher order thinking skills (Revised)

The higher-order thinking skills are identified as (1) analyzing, (2) evaluating, and (3) creating.

Analyzing: Organizing our ideas into logical patterns of understanding

> Teacher: What sorts of support would someone like Hadfield need in order to become the kind of man he is?

Question stems:
   I wonder why . . . ?
   I wonder what would happen . . . ?
   What if . . . ?
   What could have been the . . . ?
   Could we assume that . . . ?

Evaluating: Valuing what is implicit in our thinking

> Teacher: What burden of responsibility would anyone in Hadfield's position have for the lives of those with whom he (or she) worked?

Question stems:
   Which might be better . . . ?
   Does it matter . . . ?
   Would you agree that . . . ?
   Might it be better if . . . ?
   I wonder if we [you or they] were right to . . . ?
   What is your opinion . . . ?

Creating: Constructing new ideas from what is known

> Teacher: Danger and risk are considered part of exploration. How might we live in a world without such challenges?

Question stems:
   How could we [you] . . . ?
   How might . . . ?
   What if . . . ?
   I wonder how . . . ?
   Could we suppose that . . . ?

A note on use of lower-order questions

Teachers still rely on recall and "comprehension" questions as a basic approach to teaching. That reliance reflects a concern for testing outcomes; however, heavy use of these kinds of questions could limit the opportunities for students to venture into areas that demand judgment and creative thought.

Does that mean an effective teacher should never use questions that come under the first three levels of the taxonomy? No, of course not. When such questions need to be asked, they are important. So, don't think you have to follow this schema. When questioning, you must always take into account your students' background, experience, and engagement with the material — these are allies in learning.

A Taxonomy of Personal Engagement

This taxonomy was first presented in *Teaching Drama: A Mind of Many Wonders*, by Norah Morgan and Juliana Saxton (1987).

"[E]ffective pedagogy is enhanced by context in which there is an engagement between thinking and feeling, at personal, interpersonal and intrapersonal levels."
— Roz Arnold (1998, 115)

Research has made us aware of the importance of feeling as a significant component of thinking. Antonio Damasio (1994) points out that we cannot think without that thinking being informed by what we feel, have felt, or might feel. Carmel O'Sullivan (2000) reminds us that "the context of learning is just as important, if not more so, than the content" because it provides the "framework . . . in which the content is explored and examined. . . ." (n.p.). The Taxonomy of Personal Engagement is designed to help teachers grapple with the reality of teaching a group of individual students by drawing together the intersect between thinking and feeling and how lessons unfold.

So, what is the "Taxonomy of Personal Engagement"?

This formidable title is simply a definition and extension of Dorothy Heathcote's description of levels of student involvement in any learning context:

> I must first attract their attention. If I have their attention, I can gain their involvement. Then I have a chance for their investment and from that their concern. If I have their concern, I have hope for obsession. (cited in Morgan and Saxton 1987, 22)

Every class is made up of individuals who form a community. Successful lessons depend upon teachers' awareness of the levels of student engagement and their responses to what they hear and sense as they observe the students working with peers, the material, and themselves. Through use of the taxonomy, teachers can generate and maintain student involvement in the learning. The taxonomy is the agent through which the objective world of the material is brought into a relationship and made congruent with the subjective worlds of the students. It thereby allows for the possibilities of meaning making. It is the process through which students come to control and own their learning.

The six aspects of the taxonomy are identified as follows, with pertinent questions for teacher reflection:

- **Interest:** Being curious about what is presented
  What questions shall I ask to attract their attention?

- **Engaging:** Wanting to be and being involved in the task
  What questions shall I ask to draw them into active involvement, where their ideas become an important part of the process?

- **Committing:** Developing a sense of responsibility towards the task
  What questions shall I ask to invite them to take on responsibility for the inquiry?

- **Internalizing:** Merging objective concepts with personal experience, resulting in a change of understanding
  What questions shall I ask to create an environment in which they can reflect upon their thoughts, feelings, attitudes, points of view, experiences and values in relation to the material?

- **Interpreting:** Wanting and needing to communicate that understanding to others
  What questions shall I ask to invite them to express their understanding of the relationship between their subjective world, the world of their peers, and the world of the subject matter?
  What opportunities can I provide for them to formulate new questions that arise from their new understanding?

- **Evaluating:** Wanting and being willing to test those ideas out in other contexts
  What questions shall I ask to provide them with opportunities to test their new thinking in different media?

Learning springs from the need to know. "[The] intellectually effortful process of probing, analyzing and internalizing knowledge . . . enable[s] the young to develop a lifelong, personal approach to knowing and thinking . . . " (Wolf 2010, n.p.). An effective teacher capitalizes on that innate feeling by attracting, maintaining, and satisfying the attention of learners while giving them something worthwhile to think about.

Attention — both getting and holding — is of major concern today (see Wu 2016). Many sources compete for our focus, including, at times, those from the busy virtual realm of multimedia. Yet, we know that, when students are "grabbed," even young children can focus on and engage in matters that matter. In our own experience, we can engage children and young people in playing inside a story, through work in drama, for hours and sometimes weeks at a time.

Summary example

Using a source from Brian Greene's *Icarus at the Edge of Time*, we pose questions to stimulate students' personal curiosity, empathic sensibility, experience, knowledge, and understandings with the challenges of discovery, learning, and making meaning. The questions, statements, and tasks that follow may be used for an extended inquiry-based project. The questions provide models of framing.

> As the starship Proxima hurtled through space, Icarus looked longingly at the distant stars. It was the only view he knew. It was meant to be the only view he'd ever know. He had been born on the Proxima, as had his father and his father's father (1).

Interest

Teacher: I wonder what it might be like to live your entire life on a spaceship?

Engaging

Teacher: In your groups create an announcement, headline, image, or public service statement that indicates what has happened or is happening to cause the situation in which Icarus and his family find themselves.

Committing

The quoted phrases under Committing and Internalizing come from an opinion piece by Michio Kaku titled "To the Moon, Mars and Beyond." The article appeared in *The Globe and Mail* on March 3, 2018 (pages 6 and 7).

Teacher: As government officials, you are responsible for vetting expedition applicants. What questions might provide the information you need to help select the people best suited to become part of a "multiplanet species capable of flourishing elsewhere"? You may want to consider such factors as people's professional backgrounds, genetic characteristics, and psychological well-being.

Internalizing

In quoting the phrase "ark for mankind," we are, in fact, hoping that students will question that notion. If they wonder about use of *mankind*, we will know that they are figuring out this new world of ours.

Teacher: You have been selected for this opportunity of a lifetime. What concerns do you have? What issues must you settle before you leave? What is your hope for the future, knowing that you will live and die on this "ark for mankind"?

Interpreting

Teacher: A lot of the story of our world is based on one country overtaking another — we call this "colonization." Think about that as you listen to this text:

The Proxima was on a unique quest. Astronomers had picked up faint radio signals from a planet much like Earth that was orbiting Proxima Centauri — the star closest to the Sun. Once deciphered, the radio communications confirmed what many had long thought — we are not alone in the cosmos. (Greene, 2)

Teacher: What might be the code of ethics that will guide your communications and relationships with the worlds you may come into contact with?

Evaluating

"We don't like to contemplate the possibility that in the future, beings with emotions and identities like ours will no longer exist, and our place will be taken by alien life forms whose abilities dwarf our own."
— Yuval Noah Harari (2014, 412)

Teacher: Take a moment to think about the story that we have been exploring. When you are ready, turn to the people around you and talk about the ideas that we have discovered through our work. What are some of the critical questions we now face when we consider deep space travel?

In this chapter, we provided two structures for helping us to think about thinking and engagement as foundational to general lesson planning. For each taxonomy, we also offered an inquiry-based example of questions. Questions, like students, have an active role to play in the learning that unfolds in an effective lesson. As students begin to control how they are learning and ask better questions, the facilitator can take on other teaching stances that offer rich opportunities for collaborative learning.

Chapter 7   What Do I Want This Question to Do?

Questions have a wider purpose than serving as a means to elicit replies. They enable students to bring their own thoughts and feelings into expression either through uncovering answers or through developing their own questions. Questions should not be hurdles to be leapt over; rather, they are expressions of genuine interest that demand careful listening and thoughtful attention. When teachers and facilitators focus on providing diversity in ways of thinking and opportunities for engaging through many levels, participants can own their learning.

Key Question Intentions

What we offer now is a consideration of the functions of questions as a means to guide that learning. We could ask, "What type of question should I ask?" It is, however, more practical to ask, "What do I want this question to do?" We have identified three broad categories, each with a specific intention. We outline these first and then provide a series of examples.

A — Questions that elicit information: These questions draw out what is already known in terms of both information and experience and establish the appropriate procedures for the conduct of the work.

B — Questions that shape understanding: These questions help teachers and students fill in what lies between the facts and sort out, express, and elaborate how they are thinking and feeling about the material.

C — Questions that press for reflection: These questions demand intellectual and emotional commitment by challenging the individual to think critically and creatively.

Another way to think about these categories is as reading strategies. In *Reaching for Higher Thought*, Brownlie, Close, and Wingren (1988) offer these approaches:

- **on the line:** gives the information we need from the text
- **between the lines:** helps us work towards understanding the text
- **beyond the lines:** leads us to reflect on growing meanings of the text

These categories and ways of reading are non-hierarchical. You may introduce a question from any of the categories at any time during the lesson, depending on your objectives, your focus, your students' priorities, and what you want the question to do. For example, to attract student interest, a history teacher may introduce a lesson on the causes of the Second World War with any of the following questions:

Question Category Focus

A — Information
B — Understanding
C — Reflection

- How did Hitler justify his annexation of Sudetenland in 1938? (*information*)
- When might you be justified in taking over another country? (*understanding*)
- If you were an arms manufacturer, how might you feel about the possibility of war? (*reflection*)

Equally, any of these questions would be effective if asked at other points in the lesson. They all deal with the teacher's major focus: Why do people go to war?

The functions of these categories are all equally important in the learning process, demanding different kinds of thinking. However, research shows that most questions asked, whether by teachers or students, fall into the function of eliciting information and involve taking an on-the-line approach (Tofade et al. 2013). If we want our students to think more deeply so that learning becomes part of their view of themselves and their world, we must ask questions that will help them connect themselves to the material. Questions that shape understanding call for students to go between the lines. To expand those personal connections to think about the wider implications of their understanding will mean asking questions that press for reflection and take students beyond the lines. Below we offer examples that show the limitless possibilities of questions to mediate content, process, and investment.

A: Eliciting Information — On the Line

The examples below are designed for working in group contexts. (Each specific question function follows at least one example.)

1. Questions that establish procedures

What do we need to remember so we don't get in the way of the work?
Function: A means of setting rules of behavior or reminding students of rules they have set previously

Can we manage without raising our hands?
Function: To develop discussion skills by giving the students the responsibility for the ordering of the answers

Can everyone see?
Can everyone hear?
Function: To ensure a good working atmosphere where individuals monitor the situation for themselves

2. Questions that establish ways of communicating

Would it help if you talked this over with someone else?
How shall we re-form the groups?
Do we need to make a note of this?

Function: To help students consider the most productive ways of working

How are we going to do that?
How much time do you think you need?
How can we do that more efficiently?
What equipment or tools will help us?
Function: To encourage students to develop skills in organizing time and space or method of work

Have we enough material on which to base our conclusions?
What do we need to know now?
Can you manage on your own?
Function: To establish students' engagement in the material

3. Questions that establish a positive working environment

What size of group will work best for you?
How will you arrange yourselves in the group?
Who will be responsible for keeping notes?
Function: To help students work efficiently in groups independent of the teacher

4. Questions that unify the class

Are we all agreed that . . . ?
Has anyone anything to add?
Will you accept that for the moment?
Function: To ensure that the class can move along together

5. Questions that focus on recall of facts

What is the formula?
Could you summarize the main points so far?
What do we now know?
Function: To share facts to establish a firm foundation for further work

6. Questions that supply information and may suggest implications

With all the demands on your time, can you still get the display ready?
When the principal asks you to explain the arrangements, what will you say?
Considering how tight our space is, how will you negotiate its use with the others?
Function: To prepare students to deal with a possible challenge

B: Shaping Understanding — Between the Lines

The following questions rely on a specific context. In each example, we provide a short text that allows us to illustrate a process of questioning to develop understanding.

1. Questions that reveal experience

A question I am asked often is this: 'Is it cheating to use references?' In reply, I always quote Will Weng, one of my predecessors as *The Times* Crossword editor: 'It's your puzzle. Solve it any way you want.' And is it cheating to call The Times 900 number to get answers? Well, of course, but what nobody knows won't hurt you.
— Will Shortz (2001)

- What sorts of ideas do you have when you hear the phrase "That's cheating!"?
- What kinds of experiences might lead people to behave in that way?
- What do you think Mr. Shortz means when he says, ". . . but what nobody knows won't hurt you"?

Function: To discover the personal understandings students bring with them to the content of the lesson

2. Questions that focus on making connections

When Canada was a very young country, people had little means of sending messages. Very rich people living in Quebec or Montreal sent private messengers from one place or the other to carry packets of letters to their friends. Sometimes people were lucky enough to persuade the Government courier to carry letters for them and, in spring when the hunters returned to Three Rivers, Montreal or Quebec, they also distributed news. Indeed, their homecoming was an event of great importance, if for no other reason than that they could give news of the settlers whom they had seen along the way, and could deliver messages entrusted to them.
— Moore and McEwen (1936, 76)

- How would it change your lives if you were in a similar situation where communication was so apparently limited?
- What has this source to do with the art of letter writing dying out?
- By what means could the outposts communicate with the populated centres in an emergency?

Functions: To require students to use what they know and apply it to material at hand; to bring students into a relationship with the past or future

3. Questions that press students to rethink or restate by being more accurate and specific

I believe that the whole state of higher education is going to get worse. If my subject was flourishing and the universities were being treated in a more civilized way, it would be different. . . .
— Simon Blackburn (1988)

- What do you think Blackburn means by "civilized"?
- In what ways might it "be different"?
- I wonder what specific situation might have triggered Blackburn's concern?

Function: To press for intellectual clarity when the meaning is veiled

4. Questions that help promote expression of attitudes, biases, and points of view

The Keystone XL oil pipeline is designed to carry up to 830,000 barrels of petroleum per day from the oil sands of boreal forests in western Canada to oil refineries and ports on the Gulf Coast. About half of the system is already built, including a pipeline that runs east from Alberta and south through North Dakota, South Dakota and Nebraska. The State Department is now reviewing a proposed 1,179-mile addition to the pipeline . . .

The pipeline would be a job creator, although most of those jobs would be temporary . . . [it] would support 42,000 temporary jobs over its two-year construction period . . . It is estimated that it would create about 35 permanent jobs. The report estimated that building the pipeline would contribute about $3.4 billion to the American economy.
— Coral Davenport (2014, A14)

- As a citizen and a taxpayer, what are your concerns?
- Would you rather preserve the environment and be unemployed or preserve your job and let nature look after itself?
- I wonder if it is possible to live in an area of conflict and not belong to any side?
- Knowing the benefits to the economy, if the pipeline were being built through your own backyard, how might that affect your position?

Functions: To help develop attitudes to the area of study; to present opportunities for seeing material from a variety of viewpoints and to respect the attitudes and points of view of others; to become aware of the emotional power that is attached to ideas

5. Questions that demand inference and interpretation

Digital technologies are a recent addition to the learning environment. They are useful in providing extensions of and support for science learning. They also help overcome restrictions of cost, time, accessibility and safety through simulations of expensive, time-consuming and dangerous activities. They should not, however, be regarded as a primary means of delivering science education or as a replacement for the direct investigation of natural and physical phenomena.
— Adapted from Ontario Ministry of Education guidelines (1988)

- How would you explain to those concerned about optimal student learning that computers are an important and necessary adjunct to the science curriculum?
- What might be implied by the sentence, "[Digital devices] should not . . . be regarded as a primary means of delivering science education"?
- What may be the consequences of funding these technologies on other curriculum areas?

Function: To require students to consider, justify, and explain textual statements, situations, or conclusions

6. Questions that focus on meanings behind textual content

A married couple in a Western state . . . ran a house of prostitution, using three older women whom they treated abominably. Then one Fourth of July they suddenly decided to give the "girls" a vacation, all expenses paid. Drove them to Yellowstone Park, treated them to a great time, and as they drove home to put the girls back to work, they said, "Girls, we appreciate your help," and the girls said, "Thanks."

Well, the Utah authorities arrested the couple for violating the Mann Act, bringing the women back across the state line for immoral purposes. Caught dead to rights, no contest, big fine and long prison sentences for the culprits . . . some judge wrote a most moving decision. Said the facts in the case were irrefutable, the Mann Act had been transgressed, a crime had been committed, and the punishment was not unreasonable. But, he added, sometimes the law hands down a judgment which offends the rule of common sense . . . the state could properly have arrested the couple at any time during the past dozen years for wrong that they were committing, but they waited until the pair was doing the right thing . . . bringing their girls back from a paid holiday. The sense of propriety on which society must rely had been offended. Case reversed. Couple set free.

— James Michener (1987, 173)

- What have we discovered about judges and the law?
- What is the place of a "rule of common sense" in judgments that are, or should be, based on precedent?
- What might have motivated the proprietors to suddenly decide to give the "girls" a vacation?
- What is this case *really* about?

Function: To probe for meanings essential to the understanding of the material

C: Pressing for Reflection — Beyond the Lines

Here we offer texts that invite you to consider ways your questions might extend and deepen understanding.

1. Questions that develop suppositions or hypotheses

MAN BITES DOG!
— Newspaper headline

- I wonder what drove the man to bite the dog?
- Suppose the man is discovered to be a veterinarian — what then?
- What might the neighbors be saying?

Function: To provide students with opportunities to think creatively about the facts

2. Questions that focus on personal feelings

"This is our train, Marianne," Miss Randolph says, and Nora clutches at my hand. A conductor comes along the platform. "Are these the orphans, ma'am?" he asks.

Miss Randolph stands very straight. "Fourteen of them."

"We put on a special coach for you at the back," the conductor says.

The big boys carry the trunks and we take the rest of the bundles. Miss Randolph brings the emergency bag. This past week I watched her pack it with washcloths, medicine, and larkspur in case there are some stowaway fleas. None of us from St. Christopher's has any, of course. But those from the other homes and from the streets might.

"Going for a placing-out, are you?" the conductor asks Nora. "My, you look nice!"

Thank you," Nora says. She's only five, but at St. Christopher's they teach us manners early.

"Good luck!" he says to me. "I hear there are still a lot of people in the New West wanting children to adopt."

"Yes indeed," Miss Randolph says.

"We're not seeing as many going this year as last, though," the conductor adds.

"1877 was a peak year for orphans."

We go aboard.

— Eve Bunting (1996, 1)

- As a child in this situation, what would you want to make sure to bring with you?
- What were your thoughts as you read or heard this passage?
- What might be some of your hopes as you prepare to embark on this new stage of your life?
- For all of us, even a small change can be a big challenge. I wonder when you might have experienced that kind of change?

Function: To give practice in the expression and sharing of personal feelings

3. Questions that focus on future action or projection

We have found that this poem, edited for length, is a wonderful piece of material with enormous appeal for students from about age 10 on.

Kill Ra: eat inside his head,
        see with his inside eye.
A cloud covers the moon: I nod my head
We to sleep again: she smiling.
At light, Ra and I to shore
        looking for broken branches waves sometides leave us.
I say, "go this way." He say, "No, that way."
Again he find, I nothing.
With stick Ra found, I kill him.
With pebble on beach, break his skull open,
Eat his soft eye.
I walk back slowly,
Now Ra faster than me.
I see picture of his woman saying why? why?
Now Ra's inner tongue tells me to say:

"The waves took him."
My woman smiles. I sit in the sun.
Now with Ra's eye inside of me I see:
Night darker than darkness,
      darkness she cannot see.
— Ronald Duncan (from *Man*, canto 39)

- What might happen when the speaker next searches for food?
- How may what the last line says affect his woman?
- What meanings could words such as *salvation* and *punishment* have in a poem like this?

Functions: To look at implications of actions through conjecture; to experience cause and effect; to deal with what is as the basis for conjecture

4. Questions that develop critical assessment or value judgments

Just as the California Gold Rush sent millions of prospectors . . . and settlers to the West, the coming space gold rush may accelerate our expansion into the universe . . .

   The Breakthrough Starshot program has raised US $100-million and envisions sending a spacecraft to the nearest star, Proxima Centauri, which is about four light-years from Earth. But instead of sending a huge starship, . . . the plan is to send computer chips that can travel at about 20 per cent of the speed of light. These chips would be attached to parachutes, which would be inflated by 100 watts of laser power. When boosted to such fantastic velocities, they could reach Proxima Centauri in about 20 years. What is interesting about this proposal is that one can use off-the-shelf technology to reach the stars. Also, Proxima Centauri is orbited by an earth-size planet, which makes it an obvious destination for any starship . . . to "make the capability of human travel beyond our solar system a reality" in the next century.
— Michio Kaku (2018, 7)

- What information would you want to include in a computer chip to convey to other forms of human life the significance of human life?
- Given our present problems with pollution and waste disposal, how can we justify the amount of material we have left to float in space?
- What would lead you to advocate for pursuing research into the possibilities of life in outer space?
- Where would you place the value of the space program in relation to the needs of developing countries?

Functions: To require students to look at their value systems; to find ways of balancing feelings with intellectual or artistic analysis

The Agents by Which Meanings Are Mediated

Education is a process of inquiry. Whether questions are used to further discussion, promote research, prompt summaries or reflection, focus the intelligence of the group, generate a collective emotional perspective, foster shared contexts and joint understandings, offer springboards to

Using a piece of fictional text under study is a wonderful way to help students take ownership of the source and become their own questioners. See the student line master "Question Making through the Categories," which appears as an appendix on page 106. Although this lesson may be offered to individuals or pairs, it may prove richer for students to work in groups with many opportunities to build their classroom of inquiry through whole-class sharing.

new knowledge, invite student participation, encourage humor, present different ways of communicating, or provide a means of handing over control and initiating ownership, they are the chief agents by which meanings are mediated.

To that end, in Chapter 8 we provide a glossary and analyses of questions to allow teachers and facilitators to move beyond what has become for many of us a standard pattern of questioning. We do this to encourage the deeper thinking and elaboration that lead to a richer sense of the ownership of learning. In the meantime, we offer a reflection tool, below.

Why Do Teachers Ask Questions?

Traditionally teachers have used questions to check attention, assess rote learning, test knowledge, control topics of discussion, and direct students' thoughts and actions (Edwards and Mercer, 1987). When we think only in those terms, though, we limit ourselves and our students. The checklist below offers an opportunity to reflect on why we ask questions.

Do we ask questions . . .

☐ because we believe that the more questions we ask, the more possibilities there are for learning?
☐ because our view of ourselves as professionals endows us with the right and responsibility to ask questions and our view of our students grants them the right and responsibility to give answers?
☐ because we feel more comfortable when we are talking?
☐ because we have read that a good teacher asks questions, so we assume that by asking lots of questions we will be better than just "good"?
☐ because our questions are as life jackets and without them we would drown?
☐ because the more questions we ask, the more hope we have for coming up with a good one?

Questioning is far too valuable a technique not to know its purpose; each question has the potential to make a difference in the mind of a student.

Chapter 8   A Glossary of Questions

Many questions have different names for the same or similar functions. You may know different names for the questions we will describe because you have read different books and been taught by different teachers. And some questions by other names will be familiar to you from previous chapters.

Common Kinds of Classroom Questions

The **closed question** asks for a short, right answer, generally "yes" or "no" or *mumble, mumble* (translation: "I don't know"). It may be recognized by use of the interrogative structure of verb–noun, for example, "Is it?" "Have you?" "Will you?" "Shall we?"

The **open question** suggests that the teacher does not have one particular answer in mind but invites students to consider many possibilities. This kind of question is "open" to many answers.

The **polar question** asks a question to which the answer must either be yes or no, true or false. It is used extensively in questionnaires that are designed to polarize or unify opinion; there is no chance to respond with "maybe," "sometimes," or "it depends."

> Is butter bad for you?

The **branching question** gives students a choice between alternatives.

> Shall we do this . . . or that . . . ? Shall we get help or try it on our own?

The **confrontational**, or **tough**, **question** strives to eliminate inconsistency and challenges the validity of what has been said or done. It questions a student's thinking when the need for clarification arises.

> You said that the salmon streams should be protected. Now you say that B.C. Hydro should be allowed to build dams wherever there is a need. How do you explain this contradiction?

As for the **deductive question**, the common understanding is that the statement related to the question has to be accepted and the answerer's job is to prove it.

> Cinderella is a classic fairy tale. What are the characteristics of such a fairy tale?

"Without a meaningful context, students, especially younger students, may have difficulty accessing the broader possibilities and implications of an open question."
— Diane Harris (2006)

On the other hand, the **inductive question** requires the answerer to consider a series of instances and encompass them in the response.

> What are the characteristics of a classic fairy tale?

To clarify: The *deductive* question confines the area of inquiry; it narrows down the possibilities. The *inductive* question widens the process of inquiry; it is expansive and offers a panorama of possibilities. If, as Francis Hunkins (1974, 9) says, "inductive and deductive thinking are complementary parts of a continuous cognitive process," then it becomes important to know which you are using and why you are using it. Questions that require a written response tend to be deductive because the answers are easier to assess. Such questions must be carefully planned because if they are ambiguous, you won't be there to rephrase them. Written questions usually follow the statement–question format:

> Caesar was said to be ambitious. What evidence in Shakespeare's *Julius Caesar* do you have to support or refute this statement?

The **heuristic** (interpretive), or **creative, question** guides students to discover the answers for themselves using all their resources — knowledge, experience, imagination, and feelings.

> Now that we all know the facts about our situation, what are the implications for each one of us?

The **freeing question** clearly signals that there is no one right answer.

> I wonder what happened to unicorns . . . ?

The **hypothetical question** frees responders to let their imaginations run wild.

> What would you do with a million dollars?

The **divergent question** invites many different responses from numerous students and encourages both concrete and abstract thinking.

> What might happen in a hospital if the water system became contaminated?

The **research question** not only invites participants into research, but also invites them to assume responsibility for designing the procedure for the research.

> How could we find out how to measure Earth's weight?

The **probing question** asks students to think more deeply about the reasons they hold certain assumptions.

> I wonder if you could tell us a little more about why you think that might be a problem?

The **rhetorical question** is designed to affect feeling and thought — no answer is expected.

> Who among you has not sinned?

The **wondering question**, like the rhetorical, is left to hang in the air; it evokes feeling and thought and implies that the thinking about the question is more important than the answer. It is often prefaced with the phrase, "I wonder . . . ?" or "Do you suppose that . . . ?"

> I wonder what might cause a family to send their child away?

The **following question** (Graves 1983) is also known as the *mirror question* (Brooks and Emmert 1976). It reflects what has just been said so that the student can hear or understand what she or he has just said.

> Student: I don't see why we spend all this money on recycling.
> Teacher: So, you think recycling is a waste of money?

Try to avoid correcting, changing the language, or infusing your own biases into the question by your tone of voice. Note that this "mirroring" technique is used extensively in counselling.

The **clarifying question** invites the student to elaborate on a somewhat bald statement or to refine a rather ambiguous or unclear comment.

> Can you be more specific?
> I wonder why you might think that?
> I don't quite understand what you mean. Perhaps someone else could help me?
> I wonder if there is another way you could put that?
> Am I right in thinking . . . ?

The **evaluating question** invites students to look at their work in a critical fashion.

> What did you learn from this?
> What were you good at?
> What new skills have you acquired?
> What did you need help with?
> How does this compare with your work last term?
> How valid are our conclusions?

The **silly question** is not often asked because the potential asker worries about how others will react. If you need to know something, you are silly not to ask the question that will help you to find out. In fact, "silly" questions are important for all of us to ask. How relieved we feel when someone takes the risk to ask a "silly" question to which we are longing to know the answer but couldn't figure out what to ask!

The **"stupid" question** is that question which someone has the courage to ask but lacks confidence in doing so. It is generally prefaced by the phrase "I know I sound stupid, but . . . ?"

Another kind of "stupid" question is sometimes asked by the teacher. It has such an obvious answer that students can't believe it is being asked!

> Is it better to tell the truth or to lie?

While they search madly for some other answer, the teacher is left wondering why the question is so difficult. It is only later that the teacher may realize that the question was truly stupid and that the students were too polite to say so.

56

Questions to Use with Care

Now we come to a series of questions that need a great deal of thought if you intend to use any of them. The questions that follow can be deliberately designed to elicit a specific answer or to challenge something. Others we have included because they are so often asked without the asker being aware of how confusing they can be to answer.

The **leading question** is one that tells, strongly implies, or prompts the answer that is being sought. Most often, it uses the closed structure.

> Would you not say that the fog made it difficult to accurately identify the alleged assailant?

A **loaded question** is designed to access feelings in such a way that the respondent is caught in a dilemma from which it is difficult to escape. As the descriptor indicates, loaded questions carry heavy emotional weight and are designed to deepen thought. As challenges, they should be used carefully:

> I wonder, then, just what *is* your definition of patriotism?

The **serialized**, or **machine gun, question** gives students no opportunity to think independently before alternatives are thrust at them.

> If you were going to university, would you enroll at Queen's? How about York? Or Western? Or Simon Fraser?

The **marathon question** is long and involved, and students often lose its thread. The questioner may not have fully thought out how to construct the question and is trying desperately to ensure that there *is* a thread.

> What do you think we should do about free trade — keep out competition from other countries by raising tariffs on their produce, even if this means we don't have as much foreign trade — or try to increase our trade with other countries by agreeing with them to lower our tariffs if they lower theirs?

The **ambiguous question** leaves students unsure of what to reply to or how their answers will be interpreted. The main part of the question is often followed by the words "or not."

> Do you think Canada should supply arms to developing countries or not?

If the student says, "yes," does it mean "Yes, I think we should," or "Yes, I think we shouldn't"? This question is closed, not open. Tagging on "or not" just makes it impossible to answer (although students will still try).

The **double-barrelled question** is one where a bias (generally subconscious) intrudes on the question.

> Which kind of story appeals to you: one that is short and well written or one that is long and frivolous?

Your students may prefer something short and frivolous!

Watch any courtroom drama on TV to discover how a leading question is used and how often the lawyers get away with it.

The **prompt,** or **elicitation, question** is accompanied by heavy clues that are to be found in the wording of the question, the intonation, or the pauses to be filled in by students:

> This is a . . . ?
> The knife is . . . [*sharp, indrawn breath*] . . . ?
> We should remember to be . . . ? . . . when we are using knives.

Edwards and Mercer (1987) warn us that the problem with questions like those above is "that they can give a false impression [to the teacher] of the extent to which the students understand what they are saying and doing" (105).

A **contrapuntal question** is best explained by the following example:

> James, you remember that experiment, the one I was referring to, not the one in January — that was a mistake on my part — the one in February, the experiment which is referred to in your text? You know the one I'm talking about, there's no mistake about it, is there? Now, during that experiment there were three of you present — you, Pam, Ricky and Leslie — no, that makes four, I'm sorry. There were four people present and what I want to ask you, James, is did any of you during that experiment — any one or more of you, I mean you or Pam or Rick or Leslie — I think there was no one else present. Now, James, this is very important. I shall make a note of your answer. Did you, or Pam or Rick or Leslie — anyone of you, I mean — write anything like this? I don't mean the actual words — no one expects you to remember the exact words all that time ago, but anything of the kind, I mean? I'm waiting for your answer, James.

The **why question** is the great educational question. It is one of the first questions that a child will ask. It is the way in which we learn as it drives us to discover our world. For teachers and facilitators, however, there are a number of reasons for its more judicious use: the *why* question can be perceived as a tool that suggests prying, disapproval, or criticism, or it can indicate that only one response is correct.

> Why would you say that? (prying into personal life)
> Why did you do that? (criticizing personal choice)
> Why did so many people choose to immigrate at that time? (suggesting that there is only one answer)

We all ask *why* questions, but it is the *tone* in which a *why* question is asked that changes it from a perceived personal interrogation of the respondent to a reflection of a genuine need to know on the part of the questioner. A *why* question can be softened with the addition of "I wonder" before the word "why," which opens up possibilities for consideration.

Essential Questions

And then there are **unanswerable**, or **eternal, questions** of existence: Who am I? Why am I here? What is truth?

These are some of the "essential questions" that Howard Gardner (1999) lists in *The Disciplined Mind*. They are the questions of the young child, posed most often "in the language of fairy tales, myths and pretend play" (216), but they are also questions of great interest to adolescents and are usually initiated by them when the context is right.

If someone asks this type of question, it is a signal to those questioned of an ability and a need to reason in abstractions. Northrop Frye (1988) writes, "[The philosopher Martin] Heidegger says the first question of philosophy — and the hardest to answer because it's also the simplest — is: 'Why is there something rather than nothing?'" (192).

Recitation as a classroom procedure

Before we leave these definitions of questions, there is one other term for you to think about. **Recitation** is a classroom procedure in which the teacher asks a question, the student gives an answer, the teacher evaluates the answer and, in the same breath, asks another question.

Teacher: Why did people decide to leave at that time?
Student: There was a war going on?
Teacher: Could be one reason. Anyone else? Brianna?
Brianna: Food was scarce?
Teacher: Good! What preparations did they have to make . . .
And so on.

In this procedure the teacher controls the discourse; little time is given for considering the answers, and the constant evaluation of answers can be extremely inhibiting. Repeated questions addressed to a variety of people can also suggest that the first answer is wrong and lead students to change their answers. If the answer is correct, but you are looking for expansion, say so: "Would someone else like to expand on Bethany's answer?" Repeated questions can also suggest that the teacher or facilitator has an answer in mind and is trying to access it through this kind of interrogation. The questioner may keep going until hearing the desired response.

Alternatives to Questions

In *Better Answers: Written Performance That Looks Good and Sounds Smart*, Ardith Cole (2002) describes some statements as "inside-out questions" that need to be considered in the same way as questions (16).

Statements often take the place of questions and, indeed, are valuable additions to a questioning repertoire. They work extremely well, provided that students understand that a statement is offered as an invitation for discussion. Cole (2002) points out that elementary students who have little experience with statements can become confused, as they tend to see a statement as something that cannot be disputed.

A **declarative statement** is used to express a thought and to generate an exploration of that thought. It conveys information, and it does not prescribe the kind of response expected.

> I see no reason why 15-year-olds can't be recruited to fight for their country.

A **reflective restatement** is used to summarize and synthesize what a speaker has just said. It can be used to encourage students to elaborate upon their original contributions and as a way of suggesting that, if there is a misunderstanding, it is on the part of the listener rather than any inadequacy or confusion on the part of the speaker. A reflective restatement often begins with phrases such as "I understand you to say that . . . ," "You mean that . . . ," "What you are saying is . . . " Note the teacher's reflective restatement in this exchange:

> Student: Well, like it seems to me that . . . I mean there are some things that people shouldn't be allowed to pass on — like this friend of mine who got a kind of blood poisoning in hospital, you know . . .
> Teacher: You are saying that we need more efficient ways of analyzing blood.
> Student: Well, maybe. But what I was really meaning was that people with these kinds of diseases should be isolated.

This teacher's reflective restatement enabled the student to clarify for herself and for the group what she really meant.

A **state of mind statement** expresses what someone is thinking or feeling. It often begins with phrases such as the following: "I'm not sure I am coping with . . . ," "I don't feel comfortable with . . . ," "I'm not sure I know enough about . . ." It allows students to see that the teacher is capable of doubt and it models the place of uncertainty in learning. Most important, it removes the teacher from being the one with all the answers and invites students to elaborate, to help, even to direct.

An **invitational statement** invites students to elaborate: "I'd like to hear more about . . ." or "I'd be interested in knowing . . ." It demonstrates the teacher's personal interest in students' contributions.

And then there is always "the other way around" — the **instruction that masquerades as a question**: "Shall we get into groups of four?" Question-statements or question-instructions are widely used when a teacher wants to appear democratic; however, there are consequences, notably the possibility of non-compliance. "Groups of four, please" is faster, cleaner, and more to the point.

Wait for students' contributions

Questions do not operate in a vacuum. Whatever question you ask, whatever its kind and function, be sure to think about how it will help participants engage in and with the material.

You and your students need to work with an open agenda, where they see that their relationship with you is collaborative and that teaching is about negotiating shared meanings and understandings (Edwards and Westgate 1987). This kind of teaching can be a lengthy undertaking: it takes time for students to accept that without their contributions, the work cannot proceed. It is a process in which you must be prepared to wait for responses because thoughtful answers require time.

A Good Question Is an Effective Question

Let us now examine the characteristics of effective questioning through a historical example. The lesson focused on striving against great odds and not winning the prize. It served to introduce high-school students to a history of exploration.

> Captain Robert Scott and his party of five left base camp in Antarctica in October 1911, with motor sledges, ponies and dogs, in their bid to be the first at the South Pole. The motors soon broke down, the ponies, unable to cope with the extreme cold, were shot and the dogs were sent back to base because Scott was not prepared to sacrifice them. The polar party, themselves pulling the sleds, arrived at the Pole in January 1912, to find that they had been forestalled by the Norwegian explorer, Roald Amundsen. The weather on the return journey was exceptionally bad. Evans, the group doctor, died and Captain Oates sacrificed himself by walking out into a blizzard while his companions slept. The three survivors struggled on but were confined at their next camp for nine days by the blizzard. All perished. Their frozen bodies were found by search parties in November 1912.

- A good question is an expressive demonstration of genuine curiosity; behind every question there must be the intention to know.

  I wonder what drives men to risk their lives in such adventures?

- A good question has an inner logic related in some way to the teacher's focus and the students' experiences.

  When Scott saw the Norwegian flag at the South Pole, what might have been in his mind? in the minds of his men?

- In a good question, the words are ordered in such a way that the thinking is clarified both for the students and the teacher.

  What do you think their chances might have been had they kept the dogs instead of pulling the sleds themselves?

  This was a perilous expedition. How might personal biases have affected the decision making?

- In a good question, the intent must be supported by intonation and non-verbal signals. The pace of the question should match the intent. Consider these alternatives:

  Teacher (*bright and sparkling, speaking quickly*): Captain Oates chose to leave his companions asleep as he walked out into the blizzard. I wonder why he would do a thing like that? *Or*
  Teacher (*speaking slowly and almost to herself*): I wonder . . . why Captain Oates . . . would do a thing like that?

Can you hear the difference?

- A good question can provide surprise. Students will sometimes respond to one by talking about things that neither they nor the teacher were aware that they knew.

  I wonder what it must be like to risk someone else's life?

- A good question challenges existing thinking and encourages reflection.

  In your own life, who would you consider to be a hero? What makes a hero?

  If it is important for us to have models of heroism, I wonder how it is possible for someone who creates the illusion of heroism to be called a hero?

- A good question is seen as part of an ongoing dialogue which involves relationships between speakers.

  John has just suggested they should have used cellphones. What might be some problems with that suggestion?

In summary, a good question has reason, focus, clarity, and appropriate intonation. It can challenge and surprise, but it should not be seen as a means of diminishing student contributions. A good question maintains student engagement, stimulates thought, and evokes feelings. Discourse, however, is not just about the act of talking, of asking good questions — talk goes nowhere without a responsive listener.

Chapter 9   Building a Community of Inquiry

Classroom interaction is the activity that sets students into the process of inquiry — thinking, feeling, listening, responding, discussing, arguing, philosophizing, and more. According to the classic concept, learning occurs when the teacher asks questions followed by students' answers; however, the reality is that learning does not occur until learners need to know something. Although the teacher may be the initiator of the action, it is the classroom environment that encourages and supports a community of inquiry.

The teacher's job is to open doors: to let students know that doors exist, that there are many doors, that the doors are meant to be opened (some easily, some with difficulty), and that beyond every door there is something worth knowing. When something is put into words, it promotes control of the knowledge expressed. Questioning generates talk and communication that lead to learning, questioning reveals to the teacher the readiness of students to take control, and questioning by both students and teacher establishes the nature of communication in the classroom. It is the nature of the discourse that determines the quality of the learning.

Enabling Free Flowing Talk

Most important, in a community of inquiry there is the *expectation* that students will talk to one another and that the teacher will participate in that conversation, but not filter it. But what does this kind of classroom look like? The basic difference between many people engaged in social conversation and students engaged in traditional educational discourse is organization. If the desks are set in rows, the chairs need to be free, so that they can be moved. Or, desks can be arranged in pods of four to six. Alternatively, students can work at round or Harkness tables.

These kinds of configurations invite thinking and allow for free flowing conversation in a situation that becomes more social than didactic. Everyone needs to be able to see, hear, and make eye contact with one another. In these setups, participation is both encouraged and made easier. Furthermore, the facilitator is free to catch students' eyes to invite responses non-verbally.

When the teacher moves away from the traditional Western approach to classroom control, it encourages and supports dialogue between and among students. It fosters a different kind of classroom conduct marked by shared responsibility, respect, and attention.

What Exactly Is "Discourse"?

Discourse is informal talk with a flexible structure. It is generally centred around a topic or theme, but the outcome may be inconclusive.

The Harkness Table

The Harkness table, or method, is a teaching and learning approach where students sit in a large, oval configuration to discuss ideas in an encouraging, open-minded environment. There is only occasional or minimal teacher intervention.

Ways to Open and Deepen Conversation

Sharing the responsibility for learning does not mean that you are teaching less; rather, it means that you are finding opportunities both to open and deepen the conversations. It is here that you have an opportunity to **elevate language**, modelling a variety of language uses without seeming to be critical or correcting. Students can think in complexities but may not have the language that reflects that complexity.

> Teacher: In the history of maritime disasters, why might the *Titanic* have such prominence?
> Student: Because it was a major screw-up!
> Teacher: Yes, it was viewed as a tragic catastrophe caused by natural impediments combined with human errors.

As facilitator, you have an opportunity to **pick up on a remark that has a potential value.**

> Student (*to another student* sotto voce): History seems to be made up of a lot of failures.
> Teacher: I wonder if it is possible that we learn more through our failures than through being successful?

Here we are not only drawing attention to what might be a casual comment but also broadening the implications of that remark as it may be generalized.

Despite our best efforts to create a respectful listening and responding community, there are times when we will have to deal with **a response that downgrades** another's contribution.

> Student: Aw! That's stupid!
> Teacher: I wonder if there isn't something in what he just said? I wonder if you have a different idea? Wait a minute. We are just brainstorming here.

If a remark is truly offensive, it will be due to thoughtlessness, inattention, or the desire to disrupt. Deal with it accordingly.

As facilitators, we want to ensure that participants have opportunities to **rethink or restate a response.**

Some prompts:

- What made you change your mind?
- How does that fit with what was said earlier?
- In light of what we have now heard, is that still your thinking?

Think carefully about question direction

Targeting has acquired a bad name as it is often used as a control — "You're fooling around; pay attention by contributing!" It is also used as a means of ensuring that everyone on the class list answers a question in turn. There is nothing wrong with directing a question at an individual or a small group if you have a specific reason for so doing. Perhaps you are aware that Ava knows something of value from which all could benefit, or, as you asked the question, you may have noticed that Liam wants to answer. Perhaps you saw that Taylor is nodding off and needs a

These questions can also provide an opportunity for "side chat," where students turn to the person beside them and talk. Students gain a time to check-in and try out some thoughts privately before offering them to the group.

wake-up call, or you know that the students in this group need one another's support as they answer.

Thinking carefully about question direction can help us to move beyond teacher bias and student expectation. The keys for unlocking general discussion are to support all students who need assistance, encourage the students who are trying, see the potential for learning from contrary opinions, and appreciate the contributions of high academic achievers and any offer that enhances the conversation.

Effective Classroom Discussion: Characteristics

Productive classroom discourse allows students to make connections with their own lives and to take responsibility for the organization of that discourse (who speaks and when, who asks questions, and so on). "This important mode of learning," as James Britton (1970) refers to it, allows participants to help control the ideas that are introduced and developed.

A positive climate for thinking and talk

- Thought shapes language and language shapes thought, and both are necessary in the cognitive, social, and emotional development of students. Out of their shared contexts, students build "joint frames of reference," as Derek Edwards and Neil Mercer (1987, 65) put it.
- Discourse can give students practice in creating questions and assessing their impact. It is an opportunity for them to control and direct the exchange of ideas. Within the larger discourse, small natural conversations will occur; these are an important means of scaffolding as students construct their understanding by building on peer and teacher input.
- The rhythm of the dialogue is much like the rhythm of the students' own peer talk. This talk "rests upon a general consensus of opinion and attitude, yet individual differences are expressed. It is exploratory . . . it penetrates deeper . . . than a more structured, more objective analysis could have taken them" (Bruner 1982, 243).

Productive discourse can have a spill-over effect, with the participants continuing to talk outside the classroom, with you, other teachers, parents, and friends.

An appreciation of everyone's ideas

- Your role changes from that of the holder of knowledge and only controller of its revelations to that of a facilitator of learning. You have a place, but not a central place, in the dialogue.
- Because students have permission to talk, some ideas and attitudes expressed may conflict with and trespass on other people's concepts and feelings (and perhaps upon your own). Jonothan Neelands (1984) reminds us that a healthy community of inquiry invites *conspectus*, that is, the appreciation that every idea, even any contrary idea, has value and purpose.

- Effective discourse has its own built-in discipline. The individual feels a sense of responsibility to the group; the group feels a sense of responsibility to the individual. There is a common commitment to the task.

Active Responding

Today, social media can demand immediate responses and insist on attention being paid to them. Students are used to being connected, and the sense of alternative control that their devices give them shapes response patterns differently from oral exchanges.

Just as the art of questioning involves the ability to create and deliver good questions, it also depends on the quality of the responding process. The three interdependent components of this process are (1) listening, (2) thinking, and (3) hearing one's own answer. Effective questioning and responding, as in an oral conversation, demands *active* listening, *thoughtful* answers, and, of equal importance, *enough* time to think about a response as well as sensitivity to interactional opportunities as they occur (Ingram and Elliot 2016).

Active listeners are . . .

- genuinely interested in replies
- willing to be changed in some way by what they hear
- prepared to wait for answers
- as interested in the responses of others as they are in their own responses
- in tune with the social context of the classroom as well as the subject content

Thoughtful answers . . .

- depend on the care with which the questions are asked
- move the exploration on to a new stage
- raise the exploration to a higher intellectual and emotional level
- reveal the level of thought and feeling in the responder
- often appear in the form of a question
- may not come easily; may be marked by hesitancy and rephrasing (Barnes 1976)

The value of thinking time

All meaningful responses need time and it is that time which provides the opportunity to make meaning. The time between asking a question and receiving a response is most often referred to as "wait time," a phrase that signifies something very different from thinking time. Silence does not indicate that nothing is happening; thinking and feeling are internal activities that take energy and need time. In a classroom built on the principles of active participation, "thinking time" seems to describe what is happening more appropriately.

Many students are quite uncomfortable with silence. They feel that they have lost connection. Here is where the teacher's ability to wait calmly while students consider the question and formulate an answer

For a wonderfully comic and unfortunate example of any number of different kinds of questions at work all at once, see the economics teacher in the film *Ferris Bueller's Day Off*, with screenplay and direction by John Hughes.

provides reinforcement for silence as part of communicating. Waiting also gives significance to the students' thinking.

Mary Budd Rowe's 1972 research suggests that when teachers allow at least three seconds of wait time, a number of positive changes result in the classroom (see the next section). How long is three seconds? It is *two seconds longer* than most teachers wait for a response to their questions (Stahl 1994). Where is the time for students to think about answers, choose the words to frame the answers, and either give the answers or frame and articulate their questions? Where is the time for the teacher to consider the answers and formulate response to those answers? Such rapid delivery means that questions will have to be short, direct, and simple, requiring answers that are short, direct, and uncomplicated by much thought or feeling. When teachers don't get instant answers, they tend to repeat or rephrase their questions, change their questions, answer their own questions, or ask another student.

Hannah Whiteoak (2018) warns that "the nature of digital classroom tools encourages a rapid exchange of information and ideas." She reminds us of the importance of "mental incubation." Although collective brainstorming and collaborative thinking are part of our current pedagogy, often an idea brews best in solitude, notes Sherry Turkle (2015, 62). It is important for students to consider what kind of thinking they do best and where and when that happens. Both thinking in a group and individual thought are important, and it is valuable to have lots of practice in both.

The Courage to Wait

Social discourse, by definition, lacks silence, and in any conversational lull, we remember the old social dictum: keep the conversational ball rolling. We are not used to productive and constructive silences within everyday talk (Turkle 2015). Furthermore, "dead air" on the radio makes us anxious, and unless the technologies break down, something is always happening on our screens for viewing.

When a silence falls in the classroom, our natural reaction is discomfort and, sometimes, fear: fear that we have asked a poor question, that the students don't know the answer, or that the silence will act as an invitation for students to misbehave or do something irrelevant. When we *do* have the courage to increase thinking time — to wait — research demonstrates that significant changes occur:

- Students give longer answers.
- More students volunteer answers.
- Students ask more questions.
- Student responses are more analytical, creative, and evaluative.
- Students report that they find class more interesting (Ferrara 1981; Ingram and Elliott 2016).

In this age of inquiry-based curricula, it appears that over a span of almost four decades, the research still holds and should be afforded the significance it reveals.

You may want to use the reflection tool "Changing Perspectives in the Classroom" to consider aspects of your relationship with the students in your classroom. The three-page checklist is found on pages 107 to 109.

When we help our students to build a community of inquiry that nurtures conversation and engagement within a social context, we teach them to recognize that learning happens in many different configurations. As they question and respond to questions, students begin to practise leadership as a shared responsibility and to recognize that different opinions and perspectives are essential to the making of thoughtful decisions. When questions are owned by everyone, we foster those qualities of good citizenship that are central to a healthy and democratic society.

Chapter 10   Promoting Responsibility for Learning

This chapter focuses on how we can help students develop as effective questioners and better communicators. Students and teachers continue to face many pressures: personal, curricular, environmental, and, of course, achieving and measuring success. Despite these ongoing challenges, there is an ever more compelling need to teach in ways that ask students to take greater responsibility for their learning. In this fast-moving and constantly changing world, the abilities to think critically and reflectively, to listen deeply, and to cultivate resilience will enable students to "live in the present in a meaningful, sustainable, thoughtful and *pleasurable* way" (Parkins and Craig 2006, ix).

Shifting towards an Inquiry-Based Approach

With this goal in mind, we offer some suggestions that may help you to address concerns sometimes raised about the use of inquiry-based classrooms. Remember that a significant part of your job as a teacher or facilitator is to offer students and participants ways to take control of their lives: you can equip them to find the questions that will provide the answers *for* themselves and *by* themselves. Part of this process is to help them recognize that adults can be wrong, that there are answers but everyone may not know them, and that there are questions to which people have not yet found the answers.

If you are shifting your classroom practices towards a more inquiry-based approach, keep in mind the following.

- It will take time to find the techniques that work for you and your students.
- Students need time to adjust to a more demanding learning process. They need time to develop skills of discourse, to develop confidence in their abilities to work as inquirers, and to perceive that an inquiry-based approach is an interesting way to learn. It takes time for your students to accept that without their contributions, the work cannot proceed.
- Establishing the criteria for a new kind of teaching/learning process means a period of risk for both teacher and students. The signals must be clear and the agenda open.
- When students are engaged by the content and take responsibility for their own work, discipline and management problems lessen, and the

You may want to read a 2005 article by James S. Kim and Gail L. Sunderman: "Measuring Academic Proficiency under the *No Child Left Behind Act*: Implications for Educational Equity," *Educational Researcher* 34 (8): 3–13.

students themselves often resolve the problems that do occur (see Bastock, Gladstone, and Martin 2006–2007).

- Colleagues who are interested in how students learn will be supportive. You must accept, however, that those who teach to a different agenda may question your methods.
- Take time to talk to your administrators about your methods of practice so that they will know what to look for and expect when they visit your classroom. They can be very supportive because they understand the skills that 21st century learners need to develop.
- Consider working with colleagues and administrators to research alternative ways of assessing students' annual yearly progress. Multiple indicators of school performance can demonstrate students' achievements over the year more inclusively.
- Always remember the incredible value of a supportive teaching colleague.

Cultivating Reciprocity

According to the *Cambridge Advanced Learner's Dictionary* (2013), *reciprocity* is the behavior in which two people or groups of people give each other help and advantages. Think of "give and take," "back and forth," and "it takes two to tango"!

In order to encourage participation, you will need to help your students feel that they are in a risk-free environment — the environment of inquiry. Paradoxically, this environment will encourage them to take more risks and to work more seriously. It is you who models this environment. There are, however, certain common "non-facilitating teaching behaviors" (Napell, 1976) that inadvertently send negative messages which stand in the way of creating a reciprocal flow of conversation. We list these below.

Teaching behaviors to avoid

Manipulating by non-verbal signals

Students are great signal readers and generally like to please. They can — and do — change answers in response to any signals you are sending

- by facial expressions (a frown or a smile)
- by gestures (a finger snap or a dismissive turn of the head)
- by non-verbal utterances (a sigh, an in-drawn breath)

These kinds of expressions can discourage, antagonize, mock, and patronize more than any words you may say. Likewise, over-emphasized signals such as exaggerated "thumbs ups" and wide grins can seem insincere and mocking to students. These overly praise-ful actions are often aimed at rewarding certain kinds of responses, thereby narrowing the discussion rather than opening it up.

Making verbal responses that are detrimental to learning

- Being sarcastic: "Well, we do seem to know a lot about space travel, don't we?"
- Making vague and ambiguous statements: "Oh, I suppose that answer is close enough."
- Leaping to *your* conclusion:

    Student: They should have eaten the dogs.

Teacher: So, the dogs should be sacrificed?

Responding with "Yes, but . . . " or "Yes, and . . . "

>   Student: I think that if I'd been Scott's son, I would have resented that he threw away his life.
>   Teacher: Yes, but surely you would have enjoyed being the son of a hero? [Or, "Yes, and he might have lived to do other extraordinary deeds."]

In both these replies, the teacher has taken the initiative away from the student. In the "Yes, but" response, the teacher's unspoken criticism, expressed as a question, does not really invite an answer. In the "Yes, and" response, the teacher has taken over the student's idea by completing the thought. It is much better to acknowledge the answer and wait to see if other students have anything to contribute.

Giving undeserved praise

Using praise as a means of "jollying" the students along when the quality of their work does not merit it destroys the questioning process. Undeserved praise will quickly put an end to any efforts at critical thinking, clarity, and accuracy (see Dweck 2007). Students resent praise when they know they haven't earned it. Reserve your praise until it is justified. Some research even suggests that too much praise can undermine students' motivation by causing them to stop contributing for fear of failure (Brummelman et al. 2017).

Reacting to every contribution

Reacting to every student contribution with a verbal response, such as "Good," "Right," or "Well done," refocuses the attention back on you. Nothing can be more detrimental than to have students looking to the teacher for an evaluation of every response. Your attitude of interest and attention will be sufficient.

Asking questions to which students cannot possibly know the answer

>   What do you think I've got in store for you today?

Asking for choral answers

>   Chris Hadfield is a hero. All heroes are great people. Therefore, astronaut Chris Hadfield is a . . . [all together now] . . . ?

Answering your own question

>   What was the natural reaction in England when they heard the *Titanic* had sunk? Naturally, they would have been devastated, so much loss of life . . . deeply sorry for all those families . . . disappointed it wasn't the success it was meant to be.

Nothing is more frustrating for students than having a teacher do this just as they have come up with what they consider to be really good answers.

Counter-questioning

When a student asks a question, try not to respond with one of your own.

Student: What kinds of food would be taken on a space flight?
Teacher: What do you think would be suitable for astronauts?
Student: I don't know. [She wants to add, "That's why I asked you."]

Rather than countering the specific student question, you could say: "Good question, Annie. Anybody have any ideas?"

Asking questions too soon

Sometimes students have been involved in an experience at a deeply personal level. Expecting them to talk about it before it has had time to settle will be unproductive. It can also destroy or trivialize the experience for them.

Modelling

As a facilitating teacher, you have many opportunities to identify and model effective question making for your students. The statements and questions below point to a variety of techniques.

Thinking aloud

Just a moment. I have to think how best I can put this question.
Function: Modelling that the arrangement of words is important in making an effective question

I need a little time to find the right question to open this up.
Function: Modelling that any old question will not do

I know that there is a question here, but I'm not sure what it is.
Function: Indicating that not only do you not have all the answers but that you sometimes can't even find the question. This statement also offers an opportunity for the students to suggest a question.

Acknowledging contributions

That's a question that makes us think!
Function: Acknowledging a good question

I hadn't thought of that question.
Function: Acknowledging that good questions don't come only from the teacher

Hasn't this group's questions revealed some surprises?
Function: Acknowledging a group's effort to dig deeply into an idea

Encouraging students

Your questions are getting better and better!
Function: Acknowledging students' developing skills as questioners

Today your questions made us really think.
Function: Encouraging them to see that their questions are helping you learn

Reflecting or analyzing

What was the question that got us going?
Function: Helping students to think critically about questions

I wonder what made that question so interesting to us?
Function: Analyzing the qualities of a question

I wonder if there was another way we could have asked that question to get at a more detailed answer?
Function: Realizing that the form of a question controls the quality of the answer

Focusing

The questions we ask are going to be important, so we must make them carefully.
Function: Drawing attention to how the questions are made

As we are allowed only one question, what is it we need to know and how will we phrase the question to get that information?
Function: Pointing out that one question, well phrased, is better than 20 indifferent ones.

Handling an inappropriate remark

Student (*comparing South Pole explorer Robert Scott with North Pole explorer Matthew Henson*): Matthew Henson probably wouldn't have got lost in the blizzard. (*general laughter*)
Teacher: Interesting that you brought him up. Only now are we recognizing the contributions of black explorers.
Function: Defusing a situation involving an improper or unkind remark by providing new information

Helping Students Become Questioners

So far in this book, we have offered much encouragement for the development of inquiry-based, or problem-based, learning, and up to this point, we have focused on suggestions for generating student engagement and discussion. Now we turn to helping students create their own questions of substance that go beyond the informational.

"Every teacher regardless of level or subject must be a language educator," affirms Neil Postman (1979, 140).

Almost 50 years ago, Francis Hunkins (1974) reminded us, "Every time you ask a question you are presenting that question as a model to your students and modeling effective questions will help your students to ask better questions themselves" (77). Whenever students watch and listen to people talk, ask questions, and sit close together, they are demonstrating their attention and helping to create a genuine learning environment (Aker 1995). When you listen and think along with them, your students can experience the excitement and satisfaction that good questions stimulate and come to understand that questions belong as much to them as to you. As with any skill, students learn *about* questioning by practising questioning. James Moffett and Betty Jane Wagner (1976) wrote eloquently about the need for teachers to understand that language is only language *when it is being used*.

Discovering what questions do

If you want your students to examine the kinds of thinking that questions promote (see Chapter 7), we suggest that with your students, you decide on a specific topic or source.

Once it is selected, groups of two or three can make lists of questions on the topic. At the same time, you may want to build your own questions to cover the three categories in case a category is not represented.

Together, analyze the kinds of thinking students' questions produce.

EXAMPLE
Topic: Trees
Ages: 15 to 17 years old

Some examples from the brainstorming:

– What chemical changes in leaves cause them to change color?
– Pelham, Ontario, claims to have the largest maple tree in Canada. How might they know this?
– I wonder why we so often use trees as metaphors?
– How can we prevent the destruction of the rainforests of the world?

By analyzing their own questions, students will see how questions can do more than elicit information. Questions can help them to see a topic or source from different perspectives, help them to explore a variety of attitudes through their responses, and lead them to new questions.

Conducting an inquiry or working scientifically (Brownlie et al. 1988)

First, choose the topic to investigate and then with the class, make lists on board or paper that all students can see. Use the following questions as headings:

What do we know about the topic? (*know*)
What do we want to know? (*want* to know)
Where can we find the answers?
Who might help us?

Individually or in small groups, students research answers to those questions. New headings will emerge and can be listed as before.

What have we learned? (*learn*; a new version of question 1)
What new questions do we have? (a new version of question 2)

Essentially, this is a K-W-L activity.

EXAMPLE
Topic: Honey
Ages: 10 to 13 years old

What do we know?
– Honey is made by bees.
– There are lots of different kinds of honey.

- Honey is made from flowers.
- There is a queen bee, little bees, and bumble bees.
- It's sweet. It's made in a hive. In a comb.
- I've heard lots of bees have been dying.
- It is sometimes runny and sometimes hard.

What do we want to know?
- How is honey made?
- Why don't bees get sticky?
- What's the thing about bees and pollen?
- What do they eat when we take the honey?
- Is it better for you than sugar?
- Why is it called a comb?
- Do killer bees make honey?

Where can we find the answers?
- On the Internet — what key words shall we use?
- In the library: look in the catalogue under bees, insects, honey.
- Books at home
- Honey jar
- Department of Agriculture
- Television — nature programs
- Videos online — how will we search?

Who might help us?
- Louise's dad. He's a beekeeper.
- Tim's father. He works for the government.
- Mr. Southern has hives on his property.
- Mrs. Prothero (the science teacher)
- Our parents

After the research was completed, students considered these questions:

What have we learned?
- Killer bees are no different from other bees, just more bad-tempered.
- Ordinary bees don't attack unless disturbed. Killer bees will attack if they feel like it. They are not likely to come to Canada because it's too cold.
- Louise's dad gave us lots of technical knowledge: how many bees to a hive, how much honey one bee can make, and more.
- My Gran said that honey was better for us than sugar.
- When you take honey out of a hive, you put sugar in for them to eat.
- Now I understand about "busy as a bee."

What new questions do we have?
- Why are some people, like Jeanie, so allergic to bee stings?
- Was honey here before sugar?
- If it gets any warmer in Canada, will killer bees come?
- If honey is more nutritious than sugar, doesn't it harm the bees when we take it away?

And so the process continues: questions breed questions if allowed to do so.

ReQuest is a shortened form for "*reciprocal quest*ioning." Rather than getting questions from the teacher, students develop and ask their own questions of the materials under study.

Following the ReQuest procedure

This is a valuable reading strategy to use when teaching students to understand inferences in the text. Designed by A. V. Manzo (1969), ReQuest aims to help students develop an "active inquiring attitude . . . examine alternatives and originate information" (see also Brownlie et al. 1988, 81–86). The teacher invites two or three students to help her ask the class questions about the text they are reading. At the same time as they ask the question, they identify the kind of question as *on the line*, *between the lines*, or *beyond the lines* (see Chapter 7).

EXAMPLE
Topic: The story of Little Red Riding Hood
Ages: 8 to 10 years old

> Bao: Where did Little Red Riding Hood's grandmother live? On the line question.
> Alice: *That's easy. In a house in the forest. Look at the picture!*
> Mattias: What rule did Little Red break when the wolf spoke to her? Between the lines.
> Anna: *She spoke to a stranger.*
> Hassan: *And she told him where she was going.*
> Teacher: I wonder what makes children break rules? Beyond the line question.

This could lead to an interesting discussion!

Developing study guide questions

Using questions is an effective way of recalling assigned material. Students can formulate and write down the questions for which the material in their notes or textbooks supplies the answers. Later, in discussion, reviewing, or preparing for examinations, they can discover what they know (or don't know) by answering the questions.

EXAMPLE

> When the goal is to "cover" the content, efficiency and accuracy in delivery of information become measures of "effectiveness." If we ask questions we may have to "waste" time correcting inaccuracies in students' responses. If we permit students to ask questions, we may fail to reach our content goals. Yet students' "inaccurate" answers to our questions, and their irrelevant questions to us, reveal the true "effectiveness" of our "delivery system." (Kurfiss 1989, 2)

Summary question: What is the "content coverage myth," and how does it inhibit learning?

Creating test questions

Another way to help students recognize the significance of their learning is to empower them with what is usually viewed as a teacher task: creating test questions. This activity may be used as part of the reflection on the unit of study and sometimes, those questions can become the test itself. You might introduce the activity by saying:

"When we are making up tests, we need to ask questions that draw out the information we know, show that we understand the information, and give us opportunities to express our own ideas and opinions about the information."

EXAMPLE
Topic: Political systems
Ages: 14 to 18 years old

In one instance, the students in small groups spent 20 to 30 minutes brainstorming questions based on the material. They spent the remaining time discussing, arguing about, and defending their choices to the rest of the class. These are the questions they agreed on:

- What are the responsibilities of the upper and lower houses in the democratic system?
- In this country, what conditions might lead to the creation of a totalitarian state?
- Under what political system would you like to hold office?

This activity revealed to the teacher students' knowledge and understanding, served as review, and almost made the test redundant!

Hot Seating to explore perspectives

Hot Seating is used when participants have a need to expand their understanding by questioning a person who takes on a specific role, for example, the mayor in the story of the Pied Piper. Students form groups of four, and each student is identified as A, B, C, or D. They decide whom they wish to interview, for example, the mayor, the piper, a parent, a child.

Whichever character they choose to interview will require different kinds (and tones) of questions. Students need time to formulate their starter questions. Information questions may be asked where appropriate, and the questions themselves should draw out the knowledge, experience, imagination, and feelings of the person willing to be put on the Hot Seat. After the group formulates questions, someone volunteers to take on the role, and the other members become the questioners.

EXAMPLE
In a study of the planets, a group chose to interview Galileo. These are the starter questions formulated by the group:

> In what ways did you change the world?
> If you were alive today, what recommendations might you make to the space program?
> What things in your life do you regret?

After the questions have been determined, one student offers to take on the role of Galileo.

Hot Seating can be used for novel study, history, and science. It is an excellent way for students to test their understanding of what motivates people. Here, their answers are built around the material from the lesson

Two appendixes provide further opportunities for students to explore questions. Both use the nursery rhyme "Jack and Jill" as their source. One lesson is intended for primary students and the other, for older students who can question in role. See pages 110 to 111.

supplemented by appropriate imaginative responses when information is unavailable.

Using sources and games to prompt questioning

Read or see Tom Stoppard's play *Rosencrantz and Guildenstern Are Dead* for entertaining examples of Question-Question.

Letters, diary or journal entries, photographs, pictures, newspaper clippings, and math and science problems can be rich sources for learning through the asking of questions. There are also many games that use question-asking as a means of entertainment. For example, Twenty Questions and Question-Question have educative possibilities for developing questioning skills.

How Students Depend on the Quality of Our Questions

Over the years, researchers have expressed concern about the limited quality of teachers' questions. In 1976, Sondra Napell reminded us that as the quality of teachers' questions improves so, too, does the quality of the students' questions. When teachers show that they are listening and interested as they join the conversation or discussion, building on students' ideas, the students, in turn, become more engaged and supportive of their peers (Napell 1976). Forty years later, Ronald Vale (2013) alerted us to the fact that "[q]uestioning is a form of "intellectual exploration . . . that requires practice, training and mentoring" without which it will "not become an active habit of mind" (681). These two researchers are separated by more than four decades of advocating for what remains, in the words of Neil Postman (1979), "a neglected language art." We wonder if, today, there is a more positive environment for change . . .?

Inquiry-based learning has the potential to transform educational culture. The wisdom of teachers is still required but needs to be offered in different ways, as our students navigate through their increasingly complex world. The last two chapters offer lessons in which the educational focus provides opportunities for students to practise making and posing questions and coping with the challenges of dealing with the answers to their questions. Chapter 11 focuses on questioning with digital technologies and texts. Chapter 12, using the Ann Graham source, focuses on questioning and speaking and listening as a group.

Chapter 11   Questions for a Changing World: Students as Researchers

In our work with young people, we see how questions lead to the development of theories, to the testing of ideas, and to the increased understanding of worldviews and ways of being in the world. As teachers, we have all experienced the drive and engagement of students pursuing a question that is important to them. As authors, we are forever working and reworking the questions we ask. The processes for asking questions at the university level are surprisingly similar to those of our work with younger students in schools. No matter the level, we support students as they revise, rethink, and rework their questions, revisiting the questions over the duration of the inquiry. Then, finally, at the end of the process, we work with them to consider how their questions have been answered.

If there is one thing we have learned from our engagement in supporting students in such processes, it is that a good question and a solid research investigation often open more questions and that interesting answers typically open doors to further inquiries. Contemporary students have access to a myriad of different resources in their investigative pursuits, as well as access to online, digital, and multimedia sources. For these students, information that addresses their questions is multi-layered and complex, requiring new skills to process and evaluate the "answers" they find.

Our classes, both in schools and universities, reflect and respond to the changes in the world around us, the cares and concerns of children and adolescents, and the realities that face us all. In our work revising this edition, we asked ourselves these questions: What are the questions that matter to young people? What are their concerns? What are some of the big issues for their generation and succeeding generations? Although there are many matters we have observed students acting upon and working with, concerns that are connected with human impacts on the natural environment, such as climate change, species extinction, and resource management, are typically highlighted.

In this chapter we focus on student questions raised through a deep investigation of the materials that we, as individuals and societies, discard: garbage, rubbish, trash. We explore how students become researchers through their attention to the processes of questioning and the seeking of answers. We illustrate what some of the approaches outlined throughout this book might look like when presented as a unit of inquiry.

Research Focus: A Load of Rubbish — What We Use, Take, and Leave Behind

A midden is an ancient trash heap for kitchen waste, basically, a historical sort of garbage dump or landfill site. Although humans have created many middens, some animals also produce middens of, for example, discarded shells or even dung.

There is a hiking mantra, "Take nothing but photographs, leave nothing but footprints, kill nothing but time." Unfortunately, what we leave behind is too often the mark we leave on the planet, and certainly, archeologists often use ancient middens to learn about earlier societies.

As we write, garbage — refuse, waste, litter — around the planet has become a huge problem and raises many questions, not least of which is, how will people in the future judge *us* by the middens we are creating? This important topic can involve several cross-curricular areas, such as environmental science, mathematics, history, and English language arts. It can be adapted for any grade level, and this framework can be redesigned for your own classroom context.

We offer three areas of exploration:

- Investigating the Midden: Auditing the Garbage at School
- Trajectories of Our Trash: Where Does It Go?
- Raising Questions through Art: Analyzing and Creating Artworks

We use these areas to encourage students to raise questions of their own and to answer them through primary, original, and secondary sources. We also consider different ways of posing and answering questions, incorporating photography, videography, and sharing through mobile devices, as available. In reflecting on the learning, we ask students how their investigations might result in purposeful actions and how they might communicate, share, and publish their work.

Part 1: Investigating the Midden: Auditing the Garbage at School

This inquiry begins with a task designed to collect information from primary sources, by activating student thinking about the creation and disposal of garbage in our own contexts. Many schools already work towards sustainability goals, and classrooms may be set up with recycling bins as well as garbage containers. These containers can provide hands-on primary sources whose contents students examine and "read."

1. Attracting attention and raising questions (Interest)

Focus: To raise questions about what we throw away in our classroom
Materials: Classroom garbage containers; rubber gloves for the teacher and students; a protective sheet for placing the litter

> *The teacher spreads out the protective sheet on the floor and indicates to the class to gather round.*

> Teacher: We are doing something a little different today. As you watch, you may have some questions about what I am doing. Save those questions for later, please.

The teacher pours the contents of the classroom trash over the protective sheet. Some students may laugh or emit cries of disgust. The teacher puts on rubber gloves.

Teacher: Today we are going to engage in a different kind of reading. Let's read this garbage as if it were full of clues and stories. As we look through and investigate what we have thrown away, what questions might these items raise? First, though, let's sort the garbage. Who would be willing to help me do this? (*She holds up extra gloves; students volunteer.*) Thank you.

As we look at this pile of rubbish, what categories could we create to help us?

Students make suggestions.

Once the trash is sorted, the teacher invites students to photograph what they have done, using tablet, smartphone, or camera. This action documents their work, enabling the class to return to this opening activity later. In a classroom without digital photography options, students could, alternatively, create quick sketches or make a list to document the trash categories.

Words such as *interest*, *engaging*, and *committing* appear in parentheses after various unit activities. They refer to the Taxonomy of Personal Engagement, discussed in Chapter 6.

2. Wondering together (Engaging)

Focus: To record all the questions that the garbage audit raised
Materials: Sticky notes

Teacher: I asked you to save your questions as you read the trash for its clues and stories. Here's a sticky note for each of you to jot down any questions that came up as we sorted and categorized our trash.

The teacher hands out sticky notes, and students record their questions or comments.

Some questions drawn from previous work:
- I wonder how much trash we make in a year?
- I wonder how we can reduce the amount of garbage we have in our classroom?
- Where does all the rubbish go when it leaves the school?
- I noticed there was food in the garbage can. I wonder where it came from?
- I wonder if everyone makes the same amount of garbage in classrooms around the world?

The sticky notes are then collected and compiled into a "Wonder Wall."

Questions generated by this activity are just a start; more can be added to the wall over the course of the inquiry. The sticky notes can also be compiled into an electronic document that can be added to, edited, and revised. In classrooms with large shared screens (smartboard or data screens), the work can be made visible, with new questions added and color coded when they are answered to everyone's satisfaction. In classrooms without a digital screen, large poster paper might be used to keep track of the questions and answers.

Optional inquiry: Food waste or wasted food?

The garbage audit in most classrooms is likely to show food items that have been thrown away, as well as food wrappings or containers. This finding can raise questions about food waste, such as these: How much food do you think we waste over a year? How much food waste comes from prepackaged foods? How might a different kind of lunch make a difference to how much garbage we leave at school? Where else have we seen wasted food that will go to the landfill?

Students can research their own household food waste, that of the class as a whole, or that of their country. What are individuals or groups doing to address the problem of food waste? (For example, there are restaurant and market partnerships with food banks or soup kitchens.) There is a growing awareness of habitually occurring waste throughout the food chain (farm-delivery-supermarket-home). Students may want to develop a "national policy." Australia provides one useful example:

www.environment.gov.au/protection/national-waste-policy/food-waste.

3. Sorting the questions (Committing)

Focus: To recognize overlaps, similarities, and differences

> *The teacher stands next to the Wonder Wall or projects the list of questions if these have been recorded digitally.*

> Teacher: We have raised many questions to investigate. So, let's sort out our questions, looking for some similarities and differences.

> *The teacher works with the students as they decide on how these questions might be sorted.*

Similar questions might be grouped together. Some questions are factual and answerable through further investigation at the school: How much rubbish does our school create? Does our school have a garbage policy? Other questions will require library and Internet research: Why can't all plastics be recycled? What is Styrofoam made of?

4. Planning for research (Committing)

Focus: To plan together how students' questions might best be answered

With each question that the students choose to investigate, the teacher works with the students, considering how the question might be answered. For instance, the school trash policy can be checked with the school office or the principal, and the students might help write or rework a policy. The question of how much garbage is generated could be answered by checking all school waste-baskets or by generalizing from the class bin. The teacher encourages the students to determine multiple ways of answering the selected questions, the method or approach for research, and what the best solution might be.

5. Searching and citing (Committing)

Focus: To investigate approaches for searching and citing information

When each student individually searches the Internet, there will be almost as many answers as students. This realization provides opportunities to consider the reliability of sources and to refine critical thinking skills.

The teacher works with students to develop their search terms or vocabulary to be used in the catalogue or for their web browser for questions that require library or Internet research. It is helpful for the whole group to work through one question together, with all students looking up different sources on the Internet and reviewing the sources for accuracy. The teacher or students can compile a bibliographic list of all sources of information. The students, in discussion with the teacher, audit the list, determining which sources might be the most reliable and useful, and which might be the best to cite in their investigations.

By the end of Part 1, students may have begun to see the bigger picture and their places in it. They may realize that what they are learning has meaning for them. As they begin to make connections, they gain a sense of control over what they are learning, and a shift in their understanding may occur.

Using a range of credible sources and preparing accurate citations have always been important English language arts skills. These skills are more important now when even very young children are searching the Internet for information and using multiple sources for their projects. Previously, using library information, a great deal of sifting and sorting had already occurred before the student had the text. Now the search terms will determine what the student finds. Although some of the information is better, more interesting, more up-to-date, and more reliable than what was available in a limited school library collection, other information is questionable, not necessarily correct, and often misleading. Working through searching and citing with students on a regular basis will help them to develop strong research skills that utilize the easy access to information.

Part 2: Trajectories of Our Trash: Where Does It Go?

1. Making a video (Internalizing or Interpreting)

Focus: To make a video or series of photographs that capture images of garbage around the school and streets

"When education is understood as the construction of meaning, rather than merely the transmission of knowledge, the primacy of the student's engagement in the process becomes self-evident."
— William Garrison (2003, 526)

Here we begin to see the community of inquiry at work. In small groups, students take photographs or video-record garbage lying around. Depending on the age of the students, this activity may be completed with varying degrees of teacher supervision. Very young children may take a series of photographs at school, or you could go for a class walk around the local neighborhood. Parents might help their children take additional images around their neighborhood. Older students can be asked to make a video on their way home or could set out in groups from a point downtown to video-record what they find.

83

2. Sharing our journeys (Interpreting or Evaluating)

Focus: To share the images created

> *In class, the journeys are shared as students discuss what they found and the new questions that discussion raised.*

Teacher prompts:
- I wonder where that cigarette butt might end up when it goes down the drain?
- What might happen to plastic bags as they are caught by the wind?
- How does our local council deal with recycling?

3. Tracking the trajectories in and out of the system (Interpreting or Evaluating)

Focus: To follow where the garbage goes, both when it is in a bin and when it is thrown away as litter
Materials: Local council websites, provincial or state websites, news articles about international trash and recycling export, non-governmental organization features (See the end of the chapter for a list of suggestions.)

The videos and photographs have revealed litter both "inside the system" and "outside the system." The students are given choices about what they want to investigate: either garbage being processed through the local, provincial/state, national, or international systems or garbage that is out of the system. Whichever the choice, they are asked to research the route the garbage might take.

4. Map making (Interpreting or Evaluating)

Focus: To present the information found as a map
Materials: As available

Students create a map that represents the journey that the piece of rubbish they tracked might take, showing where it might end up. We would encourage students to draw or use Google maps and computer mapping tools. Older students might create a series of digital maps, looking internationally at how many richer countries now export some of their waste and recycling. Much discarded material is also now recycled. Students might look at their map as a circular journey as waste material regains its value as trade.

Teacher prompts:
- What might be the ethical implications of this kind of export?
- Children are often employed as "garbage pickers." How would we see their roles as contributing to the well-being of society? (There are multiple Internet resources pertaining to this topic.)
- When certain materials such as plastic bags and coal are banned, how else might the factories that produce them be retooled to manufacture items that would have no impact on the environment?
- How might the future judge us by the middens, or garbage dumps, we are creating?

5. Sharing our maps and possible actions (Evaluating)

Focus: To share and to demonstrate a sense of personal and collective agency

It is important that students have an opportunity to share their work publicly either to each other or to a wider audience. This sharing offers opportunities for personal and collective reflection on the diversity of perspectives and possible new ideas that have emerged for further action.
Some examples of sharing:

- Digital maps of the recycling journey can be projected on the walls of the lunchroom.
- School district offices or municipal offices responsible for recycling can be spaces for disseminating student research.
- Posters, maps, and short videos created can become sites for comment around the school.
- In class, students can present their "walking home rubbish videos" to one another for analysis of commonalities and differences. These examples are not meant to be conclusions; rather, they offer opportunities for "next steps," for action.

In Part 3, we offer one idea that moves these investigations into a wider curriculum application. Building on students' new knowledge and understanding, the ways of knowing that are in play here offer a different means of gaining students' attention; they engage aesthetic responses.

Part 3: Raising Questions through Art: Analyzing and Creating Artworks

Part 3 brings together the knowledge, understanding, and personal responses to the issues that have been raised. Art is always a container for meaning and *Six Pack Shame*, a piece of fabric art by Australian artist Linda Steele, offers a new perspective for nurturing creative meaning-making. The following activities are offered as reflection-in-action.

1. Reading an artwork (Interest)

Focus: To interpret a visual image as text
Materials: The artwork titled *Six Pack Shame*, by Linda Steele, is projected onto the wall. Alternatively, a printed, paper copy is hung on the wall or students can be directed to view it online (lindasteelequilts.com). The machine-quilted fabric art measures 100 cm by 40 cm; is made from cotton, organza, and felt fabric; is hand and machine embroidered; and is hand beaded.

A copy of the artwork appears as an appendix on page 115.

> Teacher: I invite you all to look very closely at this artwork . . .

The class studies the image and responds to the teacher's prompts about it.

Teacher prompts:
- What is it you see?
- What do you notice?

- We are looking at a photograph of an artwork that hangs in a gallery. How might it be different to see it hanging there?
- We usually think of quilts as practical blankets to keep us warm. What, for you, might be the purpose of this quilt?

This discussion is a time for students to build on what they have experienced previously and to apply that understanding to a new form. What is said in this sharing may generate ideas for responding creatively.

2. Responding to art through art (Interest and Engaging)

Focus: To create artworks that provoke questions
Materials: Art supplies, found objects, digital resources already on hand

The idea of responding to art as art may have come up in the sharing, in which case, this project may become self-generating. If not, students are invited to create their own artworks as responses. The scope of this project depends on your time and resources. There are many media that your students might explore to make a statement: they could work with the digital images and videos they collected on their neighborhood walk, perhaps writing over the images excerpts from interviews and comments, as well as adding music or soundscapes. If working with traditional materials, students might use cleaned recycling to create an image. The work of Mandy Barker or the Washed Ashore collective can serve as added inspiration. (See Resources at the end of this chapter.)

The following two activities are wonderful opportunities for students to become curators of their own work through cataloguing and displaying their work for a public exhibition. (See *Renaissance in the Classroom: Arts Integration and Meaningful Learning*, edited by Gail E. Burnaford, Arnold Aprill, and Cynthia Weiss, for further ideas.)

3. Writing an artist's statement (Committing)

Focus: To encapsulate the thinking that lies behind the image
Materials: Students' work and other materials as needed

> Teacher: In a gallery exhibit, artists have an opportunity to provide a brief statement about their work that may help the viewer understand the thinking that lies beneath the image. You now have an opportunity to create your own statement to tell us more about the bigger story you are representing through your image. You may want to begin your statement by adapting something from Linda Steele, who says, "I designed this quilt to highlight the dangers of disposing of plastic into our oceans."

Using Linda Steele's artist's statement as a prompt helps students to construct statements about their own work; they can also decide how the statements will be displayed in relation to the curated hangings or videos.

4. Exhibiting artworks (Internalizing, Interpreting, Evaluating)

Focus: To share the artworks created

This sharing could be a digital presentation and discussion for the class or a more public viewing, perhaps at a parent–teacher night with students available to discuss their work. More public yet, the video could be followed by a student led-discussion of the issues.

If space is available to serve as a gallery, you may want to approach the school or local school board offices to use it.

Further Resources: Tracking the Trajectories

ONLINE RESEARCH RESOURCES

Great Pacific Garbage Patch — Ocean Pollution Awareness
Available: https://www.youtube.com/watch?v=1qT-rOXB6NI
This resource has some terrific questions that also fit well with the "Where does your garbage go?" trajectory.

Great Pacific Garbage Patch — Explainer
Available: https://www.youtube.com/watch?v=0EyaTqezSzs
The widely watched YouTube video explores garbage sorting and classifying.

World Ocean Review: https://worldoceanreview.com/en/
This series of continually updated publications and videos draws our attention to the issues of marine science in accessible language.

GALLERY EXHIBITIONS

The Anthropocene Exhibition in Canada: https://ago.ca/press-release/art-gallery-ontario-and-national-gallery-canada-co-present-major-exhibitions
This major exhibition draws awareness to the effects of human activity on Earth. The website will continue to carry its amazing photographs.

Mandy Barker: http://mandy-barker.com
Mandy Barker is an international award–winning photographer whose work involving marine plastic debris has earned global recognition.

Washed Ashore: Art to Save the Sea: https://washedashore.org
Smithsonian's National Zoo exhibits aesthetically powerful art to educate a global audience about plastic pollution in oceans and waterways and spark positive changes in consumer habits.

Chapter 12 Unwrapping a Mystery: Students as Questioners

In *Structuring Drama Work*, Jonothan Neelands (1990) refers to the "Ann Graham" source as "a useful case study both of open structure and of the power of student questioning in constructing a narrative."

Based on a lesson by Jonothan Neelands, this inquiry-based unit is an effective way to promote student questioning skills. It involves both conducting an inquiry and role playing, which enriches the complexity of the work and deepens the students' intellectual and emotional engagement.

In writing up this unit of work, which took place over a period of a week, we have included examples of the questions asked and the ways in which they were answered. We have sought to show how the questioning works for students and teacher across the inquiry as they work together to create a truly group-authored story. We have focused on some of the details of how the inquiry might be set up in case you are not familiar with working in this way. If you have not worked in this way, we urge you to try it. The unit is designed for a general class of students with no role-playing experience. The students we worked with were aged 15 and 16.

Subject: English
Ages: 13 and up
General Focus: This unit of work provides opportunities for teachers to work with their classes to develop speaking and listening skills, and for students to work in a variety of groups of their own choice. The unit provides opportunities for students to ask questions; to listen to questions and answers from their peers; to analyze, classify, and evaluate the effectiveness of those questions; and to work as a class to build a cohesive narrative based on the information gathered. Students also have an opportunity to write stories based on their work.

Source:
In 1872, the body of Ann Graham was found by the road that runs from Ashtown to Moose Creek, as it passes the farm of Samuel Taylor. Ann, daughter of John, a blacksmith of Ashtown, had left her home some months before. No one spoke of her leaving. No one spoke of her death. No gravestone marks her burial place.

Session 1: Raising Questions

1. What can we learn from the source?

Focus: To discover what we know from the source

Teacher: Today we are going to explore the ways in which people make stories together — to see what happens when we lay our stories alongside other people's. This means that we are all going to listen carefully so that no one imposes a story on the story that we are *all* making. Let me be very clear about one thing: the story we make *is* the story. Don't come up to me at the end and say, "Yes, but now tell us the *real* story" because the real story is the one we will make. All we have to build our story from is this fragment.

The teacher reveals the text for all to see.

Teacher: Just read this fragment quietly to yourselves. (*Students do so.*) What do we know from reading this fragment?

Some examples of answers:

Student A: Ann Graham died on the road to Ashtown.
Student B: We don't know she died there. Her body was found there.
Student A: You're right!
Student C: Her father was a blacksmith.
Student D: She must have died under strange circumstances because no one spoke of her death.
Student E: We don't know that. People may not have spoken about it because they were texting all day!
Student B: Ha! Ha! There were no mobile phones in the 1800s.
And so on.

2. What questions do we have?

Focus: To sort out assumptions from facts; to work collectively; to build a list of questions that are useful, well phrased, designed to elicit information, and congruent with the period of the source

Teacher: We really don't know much, do we? What questions are beginning to form in your mind? Groups of four or five, please. Take a sheet of chart paper and one marker per group. Appoint a secretary to record your questions. (*Students do so.*) Beware of swamping other people's ideas with your own. We are working from the facts we have and any logical assumptions that arise from those facts. You have about five minutes.

Students work well together, discussing and debating the relevance, the wording, and the importance of the questions. The teacher stands aside and reminds them of time passing (which turns out to be closer to 10 minutes than 5).

Teacher: Right, everyone. Stop there. Let's hear what we've got from each group in turn. Who's ready to begin? (*Group A so indicates.*)

Questions are shared. The teacher records those questions agreed upon by the class so that everyone can see. Some examples:

Group A: How many months pregnant was Ann?
[*This question is almost always the first to be asked.*]
Teacher: Be careful! You are imposing your own story. We don't know enough yet to make an assumption like that. Can you word the question another way so that that information could be revealed?

Group A: Was Ann pregnant?

Group C: No, that's still not right. We've got a better one! What was the condition of Ann's health?

Group D: We don't know how old she was. We have, "How old was Ann at the time of her death?"

Teacher: What do you want me to write down?

Group B: Put down the one about her age first and then the one about her health.

Teacher: Are we agreed that both will be useful questions? (*Students agree.*)

This sharing continues until 15 questions that the whole class considers useful are recorded. Throughout, the teacher considers carefully how the questions are phrased. Some examples:

- Is there another way of putting that so it will open the inquiry up rather than close it down?
- How can we write that another way so that it gets at what we want to know more directly? Remember: At this point we want to keep the story very open.
- Try not to follow one storyline but rather, make these questions so that they cover a breadth of "territory."

3. Who holds the answers to these questions?

Focus: To build a collective list of the people who might help us to learn more about the story

Teacher: Read the questions carefully. Who might be able to answer them?

The class offers suggestions:

– Ann's father
– Samuel Taylor
– a religious adviser (no religion yet specified)
– a hairdresser

A student objects, "No! they didn't have hairdressers then."

An argument ensues.

Teacher: What I'm hearing is that you want to speak to someone who is probably aware of what's going on in the community.

The students identify the following:

– the barber
– the doctor
– Ann's best friend

The teacher rejects a suggestion of Ann's lover as being "I" writing rather than "we" writing: "Remember that we are building a *collective* story."

The students conclude their list as follows:

– the person who found the body
– the person who buried Ann Graham

As the roles are approved, they are listed. Now everyone can see the text, the questions, and the roles.

Teacher: Now we have eight people who might be able to give us some answers that would help us to build our story. As you think about what has happened today, remember that the story we are building must belong to all of us. Thank you for your hard work.

Session 2: Building a Story through Questioning

4. Reconnecting with the source

Focus: To review the previous day's information and set the tone for serious work

> Teacher: Please reread the source that we have been investigating, examine the questions we developed, and consider the people we decided might be able to provide answers. We need to have this information at our fingertips as this is going to be a very demanding lesson.

> *Students do as directed; there is some quiet conversation.*

5. Who will we talk to now and how are we going to do it?

Focus: To ensure that each student knows "what's up"

> Teacher: We need to deepen our understanding of the events surrounding the death of Ann Graham. I'm going to ask for five volunteers. Each volunteer will take on the responsibility of representing one of the roles we have listed on the board. (*Five students offer.*)
>
> Thank you. I am going to ask you to stand apart from us and not to talk to each other. While I know that you are prepared to undertake one of the roles listed, please do not make that choice now. I will tell you what we are going to do in a moment.

> *The teacher turns to the class.*

> Teacher: Now, we need to record the questions that we ask of those who are representing the roles on our list. Do I have five volunteers to be scribes? (*Five students volunteer.*) Great! The rest of you, please arrange your chairs in a circle. Scribes, please get paper and a pencil from my desk and then take your chairs and set them just outside the circle. (*They do so.*)
>
> I'm going to talk to the scribes for a moment. Joanne, you record the questions addressed to Ahmed. Allan, you write the questions we ask Kaylee. (*And so on until each scribe is assigned one of the role players.*)

> *The teacher then places five chairs randomly within the circle, facing in different directions.*

> Teacher (*to the role players*): You will come in when you are called and sit on any chair you choose. Once you sit, you are in role. Do not decide which role you will take now but, rather, make up your mind as you are coming in to sit down among us. You will need to listen carefully to each interview and decide what you will agree with as a fact and when you can offer another point of view. For example, if Ann's father were to be interviewed and tells us that Ann's mother died in childbirth, that would be a fact that would become a part of the story. However, if the barber says that Ann's father is a "skinflint," that is something that someone else might dispute.

The reason I ask you not to decide on your role beforehand is because as the interviews proceed, you may see that one role from our list of roles, rather than another, would be more helpful to building the story.

Teacher (*to everyone*): We are ready now to question. We will all have to listen carefully to the answers we are given because it is upon those answers that we build our story. Remember that these people have *agreed* to speak to us. I know you will treat them with respect.

6. Who will we meet and what will they tell us?

Focus: To develop questioning skills; to fold new information into old; to encourage focused listening; to work in role

Teacher (*to the students sitting in the circle*): Thank you for coming today to try to solve the mystery of Ann Graham's death. We are here to find the truth, and we have all signed the form not to publish our findings without permission.

[*This direction both suggests the teacher is playing alongside the students and suggests to the students a general role (interviewers) which sets a loose context for asking the questions.*]

Teacher: It is important to remember that the event we are investigating happened 10 years ago. There will be details that our guests will be unable to remember, things that they simply do not wish to talk about, and things that they cannot talk about.

Using a gesture only, the teacher invites someone in the "role" group to come forward into the circle and sit on one of the chairs.

Teacher: Thank you for coming. May I ask your name and your relationship to or connection with Ann Graham?

An example of the procedure:

Student in role: My name is John Graham. I am Ann's father.
Teacher: We know that you might find some of our questions distressing and that you may have forgotten some of the details of that time 10 years ago. We will understand if you do not wish to answer all the questions. This is not an inquisition. Who has the first question for Mr. Graham?

The teacher follows a similar format with the other four students who choose to take on the roles of Samuel Taylor, the barber, a nun at the convent where Ann attended school, and the person who buried her. While they are being questioned, the students in role are not to interact with one another. When Samuel Taylor makes a derogatory comment about John Graham and John Graham turns to say something, the teacher intervenes immediately, saying, "We are speaking to Mr. Taylor."

Of the 61 questions asked, about 10 were asked of each role player. The barber had fewer questions because he tended to gossip; the nun had more questions because she answered only what was asked of her. The teacher intervened seven times: asking two questions for clarification, two out of personal curiosity, and three to open up the questioning or change the pattern of the asking.

Some examples of student questions and comments on their effectiveness:

To Mr. Graham: What was your relationship with Samuel Taylor?
Comment: This is a good open question providing several pieces of information upon which others can build their questions.

To the nun: And what was Ann's home life like?
Comment: This question invites the nun to support or oppose what a previous speaker had implied. The nun responded, "I am not in a position to speak of those things." That statement is a more powerful answer than had she responded to the question directly.

To the barber: What do you think of Samuel Taylor?
Comment: The student who asks this question wants information, but the way the question is worded gives the barber licence to be creative, something that tells us a great deal about the barber, a little about Samuel Taylor, and nothing about Ann's death. When the students later analyze the questions, the teacher uses this question to demonstrate the importance of phrasing.

To Samuel Taylor: We understand from Mr. Jackson, the barber, that you have a son?
Student in role: Yes.
Student questioner: What are your ambitions for him?
Comment: This exchange comes late in the interview with Mr. Taylor. The first question is asked to check that the information previously given is correct; the second question is the key question that begins to unravel the mystery.

To the last student to be questioned: I know we've kept you waiting a long time. Thank you for your patience. What is your name?
Student in role: Mrs. Jenkins.
Teacher: Mrs. Jenkins, might I ask your connection with Ann?
Student in role: I buried her.
A student (quickly): How come a woman is burying the dead?
Comment: This question drew the story off into an interesting direction . . . with further questions asked.
Teacher (to the circle of questioners): I expect that now there are other questions in your mind that you would like to ask.

7. Checking out the story

Focus: To ask the questions not yet asked; to check out the facts that do not seem to be consistent; to weave the story more tightly

Teacher: These people (*indicating the five students on chairs in the centre of the circle*) will remain in role. You (*to the other students*) may go around and ask them any other questions that you may have. Scribes, this is now your chance to ask questions.

The group breaks up, moving around among the chairs in the centre of the circle, asking questions, or just listening to others asking questions. About 10 minutes pass.

Teacher: Thank you. We have no wish to tire these people out. They have been so kind and patient putting up with our questions. You have given us a lot to think about.

8. What did we hear?

Focus: To share what has been learned; to evaluate its importance; to try to fit it into the story that is developing

Teacher (*to the role players*): Please, come out of role now and bring your chairs back into the large circle. (*They do so.*)
　　Scribes, hang on to your questions for the moment as we may need them as reference. Please, open the circle to let the scribes join us. (*Students do so.*)
　　Has anyone picked up any new information that you think we need to hear?

Many interesting things are mentioned, phrased in ways such as these:

- I learned that . . .
- I don't understand why her . . .
- Mr. Taylor seemed uncomfortable about . . .
- I think we should all know that . . .

9. Laying Ann to rest

Focus: To place students in the middle of the story; to demonstrate multiple perspectives of an event

Teacher: Scribes, please put your recorded questions on my desk. Thank you. Everyone, please place all the chairs *but one* against the walls and stand by them.

The teacher takes the remaining chair, turns it over, and places it on the floor in the middle of the room.

Teacher: This chair marks the spot where Ann Graham's body is to be buried. Will those of you who took on roles, please place yourselves *where* you would be and *how* you would be at the time of Ann's burial. (*They do so.*)

The rest of the class watches as the picture takes shape.

Teacher: Look at this picture. If there is anything you don't understand about the arrangement, ask a question.

An example:

Student: Bill, why are you standing on that chair?
Bill: I don't think Taylor would be at the burial, but I am standing on my hill, watching.

Students question until everyone is satisfied with the picture.

Teacher (*to the rest of the class*): Now it is your turn. As members of Ann's village, take a moment to think where you might be and what you might be doing at the time of Ann's burial. (*The teacher waits.*)
　　Now, take your place in the picture one at a time. (*They do so, in silence.*)

Placing your hand with a firm but gentle touch on a student's shoulder offers a signal to speak. Leave your hand there until the student finishes speaking, then lift it with a "thank you." A tap on the shoulder does not convey your attention, and if the student chooses not to speak, you may be concerned that the student missed your signal altogether. In this activity, four students chose not to speak.

Just hold that picture for a moment. Close your eyes. (*They do so.*)

As the body is being lowered into the ground, what question is in your mind? I shall come around and place my hand on your shoulder. When you feel my hand on your shoulder, say your question aloud.

Some examples:

- What was in Ann's mind the moment she faced death?
- Why am I not allowed to toll the bell?
- Why didn't I do what I knew I should have done?
- She asked for it. What's all the fuss about?
- I wonder what the person who killed her is thinking now?
- Why?

"Why?" was the final question. The teacher left a silence.

10. What now?

Focus: To consider the story they have made together; to think about how they made the story and what helped it to grow

> Teacher: Find someone near to you, sit down together, and when you are ready, begin talking about the experience.

> *Students reflect together and share their thinking.*

We specifically omitted the choice of a digital entry to remain congruent with the time of the story.

> Teacher: We have been building a collective story, but there are still many questions to be answered. Now it is time for you to write about the story as *you* see it. Hold to the facts that have been established, but you are free to tell the story in your own way, in or out of role. You may write it as a diary entry, a letter, a short story, a newspaper article, as the summary of a trial — in any way that you feel is right for what you want to say and how you want to say it. Please have your first draft ready for next class.

Session 3: Writing Based on Information Gathered

11. What really happened?

Focus: To work collaboratively; to read their own words or those of another aloud or silently, to assess, to edit, to rewrite

This lesson fulfilled one of the teaching expectations: to provide opportunities for students to write stories based on the information gathered from the questions and answers.

Students wrote in pairs or small groups, sharing their first drafts and working as editors with their partners.

None of the students completed the assignment in class time. They finished the work at home, which indicates their commitment to the task and to the work of the previous lessons.

The writing took many forms. Some texts were on paper made to look old. Some were letters, one or two sealed with wax, and one was in the form of Samuel Taylor's will. Several texts were written as diary entries, and some were short stories.

Session 4: Examining How Questions Helped Build the Story

12. Analyzing our questions

For further notes on Session 4 and a reproducible version of the response form, see Appendix 10: Evaluating Questions on Ann Graham (pages 116 and 117).

Focus: To provide opportunities for students to analyze, classify, and evaluate the effectiveness of the questions

Teacher: I have the scribes' transcriptions of the questions that you asked or were asked during the in-role interviews. Each group will have the list of those questions and a response sheet. Your first task is to read through the questions. Choose three or more to examine closely and then decide under which category each of your questions fit. I have listed the three categories [perhaps on a chalkboard, with a docucam, or on an interactive whiteboard].

Category A questions give us information.
Category B questions have answers that fill in the gaps between the facts and help us make connections.
Category C questions invite answers that deepen the story.

Teacher: This is challenging work as questions may appear to fit into more than one category. Record your decisions on the response sheet. You'll note that I have given each category of question a letter for easy identification.

Students work with the questions.

13. Valuing and rephrasing questions

Focus: To consider how a question works and how a question might be more effectively phrased

Teacher: Now, thinking as writers, talk together about how each question helped us to build our story. Write your ideas on the response form. Finally, if you feel that the question would work better if rephrased, use the space for rephrasing. If not, comment on why the question did not need rephrasing.

The teacher circulates while students work.

Teacher: You have some good ideas. Let's share some of our work. In your group, choose an example that you would like to share with us. Tell us the question, what kind of question you decided it was, how it helped the story, and if you thought of a better way to express the question. (*Students make their choices.*)

As we listen to these questions, think about the quality of each question, how the words are put together to invite an answer, and which questions best invite you to answer.

Several questions are shared and discussed. There is a lively conversation about whether the questions made connections or deepened the story. Students conclude that, as writers, they see the value of the question lies in the connections it makes but, as readers, they feel the answer works to deepen the story.

At the teacher's request, students put the revised question sheets on her desk. The teacher later reviewed these sheets to identify if any re-teaching was required.

14. The big questions that remain to be asked

Focus: To encourage students to think beyond the story in new ways

Teacher: Find a partner. (*Students do so.*)
 Take a moment to sit quietly and think. Stories, if they are to reach a wide audience, have something in them that is universal. If you had the opportunity to ask not more than three "big" questions that would help us to see this story as more than just Ann Graham's story, what might those questions be? Who might be able to answer them? Work together and share your ideas. (*Students do so.*)

As students work, the teacher circulates. After giving a time notice, she asks students to find another pair and share their work. They do. A few minutes pass.

Teacher: There are some wonderful questions here that really open up the story in quite unexpected ways. Let's hear some of them.

Some examples:

- Some say it would have been better if she had never been born. How do you see her life and death?
- If no one ever really loved Ann, what kind of mother could she have been if her baby had lived?
- Is something less wrong simply because it happened in the past?

The whole class then moved into a discussion prompted by this question: "I wonder why some questions are difficult to answer . . .?"

This source has proved to be of great interest to students and participants in several disciplines. It offers an open structure that invites them into active participation in their learning. A similar source, "Mary Ellery: Traveler in Space," was designed for students ages 11 and up: it appears in *Into the Story 2: More Stories! More Drama!*, a 2016 title written by Carole Miller and Juliana Saxton (pages 135–55). We invite you to teach or adapt either of these structures (changing gender perhaps?) according to what you and your students need.

Conclusion: Raising Difficult Questions

A focus of this new edition has been to build on the sense of agency, of purpose, and of motivation for change that students have been developing in the last decade, in part, through their use of social media. These personal dispositions, allied with critical thinking, empathy, and a reflective stance, need to be consistently encouraged and developed in our classrooms.

Questions raised in today's climate are often difficult to answer but reflecting on them has the potential to create conversations that are thoughtful, attentive, aware, and rich in perspectives. In our increasingly complex world, meanings become more and more blurred and while there are times when no answers are to be had, being able to deal with ambiguities and uncertainty is as important as finding the questions.

Only when we are able to think critically and talk openly and empathically about the big issues we face can we see the breadth of possibilities and implications as we hear and take into consideration others' expressions and points of view. These ways of thinking, listening, and exchanging ideas are central to an effective democratic process, the enactment of social justice, the mediation of influences of social media, and how we undertake our ethical responsibilities to one another.

As we learn to ask better questions, we begin to change ourselves. One day, perhaps, that could lead to changing the world . . .

Appendixes

Who Asks Questions?

Here is a list of people whose business it is to ask questions. You may add to this list if you think of others.

interviewer
journalist
doctor
lawyer
police officer
detective
researcher
someone who has been away
interrogator

inquisitor
devil's advocate
teacher
store owner
psychiatrist/psychologist
child
politician
social worker
alien

1. a) Review the list above. Choose three questioner roles.
   b) Choose three appropriate respondent roles either from the above list or as you otherwise determine.
   c) What question will you as the questioner ask of each person?

   Example: Role: Journalist   Respondent: Famous person

   Question: When did you know that you wanted to be an Olympic medalist?

   Role   **Respondent**

   a) _____   _____

   Question: _____

   b) _____   _____

   Question: _____

   c) _____   _____

   Question: _____

2. Here is a question that we ask every day: "So, what have you been up to?" Choose three people from the list above. Determine how each would phrase that everyday question to discover what they want to know.

   Example: Store owner: Hello, Mrs. Chen. I haven't seen you for some time. Been away?

   Role: _____   Question: _____

   Role: _____   Question: _____

   Role: _____   Question: _____

3. Remember the story of Cinderella? If you could ask only three questions, what would they be, and who in the story could answer them?

   Example: Tell me, ladies, how are you getting to the ball tonight?

   Person to answer: The stepmother

   Question: _____

   _____   Answerer: _____

   Question: _____

   _____   Answerer: _____

   Question: _____

   _____   Answerer: _____

Pembroke Publishers © 2018 *Asking Better Questions*, 3rd ed., by Saxton/Miller/Laidlaw/O'Mara ISBN 978-1-55138-335-4

Building Questions upon Questions

This series of activities not only builds questioning skills but offers a way for students to engage with and own the material. Students will have to read or view the chosen text carefully if they are to make meaning collaboratively with their peers.

Preparation The class reads a novel, poem, play, or short story, or views a film, documentary, or piece of art. Each student is given a response form (next page).

Activity 1 Ask students to record on their response forms three questions that they would like answered about the text they have just read or viewed. (**Task 1**)

Activity 2 In partners, students try to answer each other's questions.

Activity 3 Still in partners, students decide on three questions for which they both want to find the answers. They may use questions they already have or perhaps new questions that arose through their conversation. (**Task 2**)

Activity 4 Each pair joins with another pair. Group members exchange questions and give answers.

Activity 5 In their groups of four, students settle on one question that they all feel is powerful enough to engage the whole class in discussion. When they have decided, they choose someone to write it on the chalkboard or Smartboard, or use a docucam to present. (**Task 3**)

Activity 6 Say to the class: "Now, we have a great list of questions. Where shall we begin our discussion?"

The questions will generate a reflective discussion that serves both to deepen understanding of the text and offer opportunities for re-teaching, as needed. You may want to explore with the students the criteria on which they based their choices of powerful questions (see Activity 8); however, the most important thing is what the questions open up for discussion (see Activity 7).

Activity 7 Invite students to take a moment to reflect on any changes in their thinking about the material. Ask them to record ideas on their response forms (*reflecting on meaning*).

Activity 8 Ask students to note on their response forms what they think makes a powerful question (*reflecting on process*).

Adapted from Frank McTeague, *Shared Reading in the Middle and High School Years* (Markham, ON: Pembroke, 1992), 52.

Building Questions upon Questions: Response Form

Task 1: List your three questions below.

Question 1:

_____

_____

Question 2:

_____

_____

Question 3:

_____

_____

Task 2: List the three questions that you and your partner have decided upon.

Question 1:

_____

_____

Question 2:

_____

_____

Question 3:

_____

_____

Task 3: Record the powerful question that your group has decided upon.

_____

_____

Reflection: How has your thinking changed?

_____

_____

_____

What makes a question powerful?

_____

_____

_____

Pembroke Publishers © 2018 *Asking Better Questions*, 3rd ed., by Saxton/Miller/Laidlaw/O'Mara ISBN 978-1-55138-335-4

Thinking as Someone Else

Throughout this text, there have been references to working in role. Although we typically think "about" someone, role enables us to think "as if we were." We emphasize the value of working in role as a means of engaging students cognitively and affectively, which leads to the development of empathic awareness. When students connect themselves with other people in this way, they are better able to develop the multiple perspectives so essential in critical thinking.

The questions on the response form help create the background and context and generate thinking more deeply about how and why things have happened, are happening, or could happen. "Thinking as Someone Else" covers all the categories of questioning and can be used in a variety of subject areas to help students consider the attitudes and points of view of the people involved; for example, as Marie Curie, students might think about the personal costs of scientific discovery. Thinking not just about a subject but as someone who undertakes that profession or took part in certain events is a way for students to develop greater understanding of the context.

How to use the response sheet:

Example: Assume that students have just completed the first chapters of a novel.

- Based on the content, students choose their roles. More than one student may take on the same role.
- Begin by having the students answer only a few questions on the response sheet. You and your students can decide on the ones they can or want to answer.
- As they continue to read, students will gain additional information and so will be able to ask and answer more questions. When the work is completed, prompt students to reread what they have written and make any changes that are suggested in light of their experiences.

Thinking as Someone Else: Response Form

1. Who am I? _____

2. Where do I live? _____

3. In what period am I living? _____

_____

4. How old am I in years? in experience? _____

_____

5. What do I do in my life? _____

_____

6. What most concerns me? _____

_____

7. What might be a central problem for someone else? _____

_____

8. Besides my own, whose story is this? _____

_____

9. What do I want now? What do I hope for in the future? _____

_____

10. What are my reasons for wanting these things? _____

_____

11. What can I do to make them happen? _____

_____

12. How do other people see me? _____

_____

13. How do I view the world and my place in it? _____

_____

Writing in role is a means of reflecting inside the work and can be done at any time during the work, at the end of the process, or at both times. It may be approached in many ways: personal thoughts in a diary; a letter to an authority or a friend; a letter to the newspaper; stream of consciousness, and so on. How it is approached depends somewhat on the context. For example, someone writing in role as a lawyer might draft notes in preparation for a trial. The answers to the questions above will serve as a basis for the imaginative writing.

Question Making through the Categories

Lesson: Based on a piece of fictional text under study, you may build the questions and share them or use your questions in a written response, such as a brief magazine profile.

1. What information is important?

   - Identify and list it.
   - Write that information as questions that would be interesting to answer.

2. Identify one character in the story that interests you.

   - What are some things you might connect with? Write, underline, or highlight these.
   - Use these words as a basis for questions that could elicit those connections.
   - Choose one or two questions that might raise your curiosity and encourage you to answer.

3. Move beyond the story. What are the questions that reach into the heart of the matter? expand the material into a wider world? put this text into a wider perspective?

   - Write one or two questions that explore or expand the heart of this story.

4. Move into the world of the character you have chosen, exploring that character through Hot Seating. (If you are not already familiar with this, your teacher will explain it to you.)

   - What questions would you have for someone who had been this character's teacher?
   - What questions would you have for the character's mother or father?
   - What questions would you have for this character 20 years further on?

5. Consider what this story is really about or, as is said in theatre, what do you see as its subtext, or theme?

   - Turn your ideas into questions or statements that might be used to attract the reader's interest.

6. Consider this story from your character's perspective. What are some things in your character's life that he or she might have chosen to change? This final question has the potential for rich discussion.

Pembroke Publishers © 2018 *Asking Better Questions*, 3rd ed., by Saxton/Miller/Laidlaw/O'Mara ISBN 978-1-55138-335-4

Changing Perspectives in the Classroom

Sometimes, it is useful to think about what is happening in our classrooms from a different perspective — to put on a different hat, so to speak. The questions and statements below may help you think about your class from "both sides of the desk." Note that it is helpful to identify the time of year and time of day because often the same activity will yield different responses.

Time frame for the reflection: _____

Subject and grade: _____

Teaching focus: _____

A. Look at your teaching from a student's point of view.

The experience . . .
☐ was so good that I want to bring my friends
☐ was okay, certainly better than a lecture
☐ was boring but necessary
☐ had nothing to do with me
☐ wasn't like any of the above, but . . .

When I look at my teacher, I see someone who . . .
☐ is interested in the material and in helping me to understand
☐ is scared of us
☐ is bored by us
☐ has lots of energy
☐ really sees me

When I listen to my teacher, I . . .
☐ am entertained, but nothing stays with me
☐ hear stories that help me to relate to the material
☐ hear stories that help me to understand the material
☐ hear stories that have nothing to do with anything
☐ hear only background noise

When my teacher walks into the room, I feel . . .
☐ a sense of anticipation
☐ ready to deal with whatever comes up
☐ confident that what happens will be important to me
☐ pessimistic about the good use of my time, but what can I do about it?
☐ a sense of impending doom

When my teacher asks questions, I feel . . .
☐ she already knows the answer
☐ there is only one right answer
☐ she doesn't expect me to know the answer
☐ my answer won't be good enough
☐ my answer will be treated with respect

Changing Perspectives in the Classroom (continued)

Questions to think about as if you were a student:

1. What did I learn and was it relevant? If I thought *no*, does it really matter?

_____

2. If I did learn something, what could I change to make the experience even better for me?

_____

It's time to switch hats.

B. As teacher, you may find the following questions useful in helping you think about the environment of your classroom and how that may affect learning.

Beginning of the class:
- What kinds of behaviors do I see at the beginning of my class?

_____

- What kinds of behaviors please me, and what kinds make me uncomfortable, angry, or sad (or all three)?

_____

- How can I capitalize on what is positive, and how can I change what I don't much like?

_____

- How much of this behavior has to do with what I am doing or have done?

_____

- How much has to do with things beyond my control?

_____

- Are these things really beyond my control?

_____

During the class:
- What kinds of behaviors do I see?

_____

- What kinds of behaviors demonstrate that my students are engaged with both the material and with me?

_____

- What kinds of behaviors suggest that my students are either not with me or with the material?

_____

Pembroke Publishers © 2018 *Asking Better Questions*, 3rd ed., by Saxton/Miller/Laidlaw/O'Mara ISBN 978-1-55138-335-4

Changing Perspectives in the Classroom (continued)

- Why am I seeing this student behavior?
- ☐ Has this behavior to do with me?
- ☐ Has this behavior to do with the material?
- ☐ Does this behavior relate to the way I am communicating the material?
- ☐ Does this behavior relate to them and experiences over which I have no control?
- ☐ Am I kidding myself?

- What sorts of questions am I asking?
- ☐ Questions that always follow from easy to hard
- ☐ Questions that offer multiple ways of thinking
- ☐ Questions that help my students relate to what they are learning
- ☐ Questions that can be answered with a *yes* or a *no*
- ☐ Questions that invite students to express their feelings as well as their knowledge
- ☐ Questions that get in the way of the learning
- ☐ Questions that allow students to reflect (and follow with the time provided to do it)

End of the class:
- What kinds of behaviors do I see?

_____

_____

- What signs are there that this has been a good experience for my students?

_____

_____

- What signs are there that this has been a good experience for me?

_____

_____

- What signs tell me I need to improve my efforts as a presenter? (Should I clarify my notes, relax, and enjoy myself more?)

_____

_____

For next time:

One thing to try: _____

Two things to think about: _____

_____

Thanks to Mem Fox whose suggestions for a language arts evaluation in *Radical Reflections* (New York: Harcourt Brace, 1993), pages 82 and 83, served as the inspiration for this reflective exercise.

Pembroke Publishers © 2018 *Asking Better Questions*, 3rd ed., by Saxton/Miller/Laidlaw/O'Mara ISBN 978-1-55138-335-4

Asking Questions about Jack and Jill: Primary

Grouping: Whole class

Strategy: Building on questions

Administration: Nursery rhyme projected or displayed so all the class can see the words

Focus: Looking for questions to build a story

We offer this activity for a primary class as a way for students to think about questions and why they are so useful.

> *Source:*
> Jack and Jill went up the hill
> to fetch a pail of water.
> Jack fell down and broke his crown
> and Jill came tumbling after.

If some students are unfamiliar with this rhyme, the teacher may need to do some preparatory work. It is always interesting to consider the word "crown," which has different meanings. "Crown" in the royal sense may be more appealing for younger children and will provide quite a different take on the story.

> Teacher: Here is the situation: Jack and Jill are in hospital. They are in satisfactory condition, but they are not allowed any visitors yet. Who might be able to tell us what happened?
> *Students make a list, which will likely include a farmer, Jack and Jill's mother or father, and a teacher.*
> Teacher: Who on our list would you most like to talk to?
> *Students make suggestions.*
> Teacher: Now that we have decided whom we are going to talk to, what sorts of questions do you have for this person?
> *Students may come up with ideas like these: What time did the accident happen? What were they doing before they went up the hill? Are Jack and Jill twins?*

This is an opportunity for the teacher to expand students' questions and possibly elevate their language (see Chapter 9, "Ways to Open and Deepen Conversation," page 64.)

Grouping: Whole class

Strategy: Teacher in role

Administration: The questions as composed

Focus: Using our questions to find answers

> Teacher: Now that we have some really good questions, would you allow me to become the person you have chosen to answer them? (*They agree.*)
> *The teacher places a chair where everyone can see it and stands near it.*
> Teacher: Who thinks they have the first question? (*Someone volunteers.*)
> Teacher: When I sit down, I will be in role as _____ and ready to answer your questions.
> *The teacher answers the students' questions, striving to create a believable story. Responses will need to build coherently on the questions asked; the length of time taken depends on student interest.*

> Teacher: Thank you for your questions and for your interest in this situation. If I find out anything else, I will be sure to let you all know.
> *The teacher stands up and moves away from the chair.*
> Teacher (*now out of role*): Well, you are certainly wonderful questioners. Sometimes it was hard for me to think of an answer. What did you hear that helped us know more about what happened?

This first experience may not take long, but it offers opportunities for the class to see the teacher in a different role — they are most likely used to seeing the teacher ask the questions. After this activity, they may want to meet someone else, in which case, they can reuse their initial questions or determine new ones appropriate to the role.

After this reflection, the students could make a storyboard, write a story that includes the new information they have just learned, or create the doctor's report about this accident — a great way to find out how much they know about going to the doctor.

Asking Questions about Jack and Jill: Questioning in Role

Grouping: Whole class

Strategy: Building questions

Administration: Nursery rhyme projected; pencils, and response sheets

Focus: Looking for questions that generate rich answers

In this lesson, we work with the same source as we did with primary students; however, this time, it is for older students who can work more independently and responsibly. The lesson involves perspective taking. It also involves becoming aware that the ways in which questions are asked and answered can influence how the content unfolds.

Source:
Jack and Jill went up the hill
to fetch a pail of water.
Jack fell down and broke his crown
and Jill came tumbling after.

Teacher: Here is the situation: Jack and Jill are in hospital. They are in satisfactory condition, but they are not allowed to have any visitors yet. To whom could we speak to find out what happened?
The teacher and students make a list of people, perhaps up to seven names.
Teacher: Now that we have our list, what sorts of questions would we want to ask these people? (*They list up to 10 questions.*)
   Talk to the person next to you about how those questions would change depending on who was asking them and who was responding to them.
Students share some of their discoveries.

Grouping: Pairs

Strategy: Questioning in role

Administration: Questions as composed, chairs for everyone

Focus: To work in role to uncover what happened

Teacher: Find a partner, and set your chairs facing each other. (*They do.*)
   Decide on the person you want to interview. (*They do.*)
   Choose who will take on the role of questioner and who will take on the role of respondent. (*They do.*)
   Think for a moment about the attitudes and points of view of the roles you have chosen. Those attitudes and points of view will help you form your questions and shape your replies. For example, if you are a social worker who thinks that the story is about unsupervised children, how would that influence the kinds of questions you ask? If you are a parent speaking to the social worker, the way those questions are asked will certainly affect how you answer. Take a moment to think about that. (*They do.*) You can use any of the questions we have created, and add any of your own as appropriate to the role.
   Decide who will speak first. And when you are ready, you may begin.
The teacher circulates, listening for questions and responses and perhaps recording some to refer to during reflection.
Teacher: Stop now. Just think quietly about what you have heard. (*They do.*)
   Talk with your partner about what made your conversation feel real and how your questions and your answers helped to make it so. (*Partners talk together.*)
Teacher (*to whole class*): What questions or answers helped to unfold your story? (*They share.*)

Teacher prompts to use during the reflections:

- What sorts of questions did you find to be the most useful?
- Who heard something that they hadn't thought of?
- Who found themselves surprised by what they were saying?

Getting Started: A Thinking Process for Teachers

The questions in this reflective tool are based on those of a handout designed by our colleague Margaret Burke. Their purpose is to help you think about getting started in a new classroom, a new position, or a new school. You might, from your own experience, come up with other questions to consider.

Purpose

What am I *going* to teach?
What do I *have* to teach?
What do I *want* to teach?
What do I *need* to teach to this class at this time?
(Social skills? Curriculum expectations? Subject skills?)

Questions about My Students and What They Know

What exactly do I know about *this* class?
What will I *need* to know before I begin?
How will I get that information?
What do I want *these* students at *this* time to know about the topic?
What might they already know about this topic?
How can I find out where they are at in relation to the topic?
What do they need to know before the unit gets going?
What exactly do I know about the topic?
What can I handle? Are there aspects of this topic I would rather not deal with?

Learning Outcomes

What do I recognize as the important themes?
How can I frame these themes as key questions or statements to guide my planning?
What are the most important learning outcomes of this unit for my students?
What other hidden-curriculum (soft skills) learning outcomes are possible?
How well do these outcomes support each other?
What could be the culminating task?

Relevance

How is this topic relevant to my students as individuals and as a class?
How can I make this topic relevant to them?

Strategies for Action

What questions or statements will grab the students' interest right from the start?
How can I best turn the learning into "doing something"?
At this time of day, who are my teaching neighbors? What is their noise level tolerance?

Focus

What is my focus for the overall unit?
Keeping that focus in mind, what is my focus for the introductory lesson? Is it interest? content? reflective questions?
What will be my reflective questions so that the students are reminded of what they have been working on or learning?
What is my likely focus for the next lesson? the next? and the next? [These cannot be decided too far ahead, but you should have some sense of where your lessons are or may be going.]
How many lessons can I assign this topic given the aspects of the curriculum that must be covered?
How can I best sum up what we have learned?

Pembroke Publishers © 2018 *Asking Better Questions*, 3rd ed., by Saxton/Miller/Laidlaw/O'Mara ISBN 978-1-55138-335-4

Getting Started: A Thinking Process for Teachers (continued)

Assessment

How will I assess the students on this material? (Will I base assessment on personal work or group work? When will I assess? Will I do it more than once?)

What assessment structures will be best? How many different kinds will I use?

How will the criteria be set? Will it be by me? by the students? by all of us?

Is it realistic to think the students can do this? (Have I given them the tools for assessing?)

Where might I look for assessment help or ideas? (Which books should I turn to? Who could I ask?)

Other things to consider:
Materials

Do I have enough backup material?

Is it the right kind of material?

Are these available? Where?

Are they available to me when I want them?

What arrangements do I have to make to ensure that they are available?

How do I access the photocopier, and how do I unlock and lock up?

Can I get more material or information if or when I need it? How quickly?

Note: It is helpful to know where things are stored and how to access them. For example, where will you find books, a CD player, a docucam, a slide projector, video equipment, computers, iPads, paper, pens, pencils, markers, glue, scissors, chairs, a table, and boxes?

Questions about Tech Use

Do the technological resources available to me work?

What are their idiosyncrasies?

Do I have the necessary keys?

Have I practised using the equipment before class?

Availability

Can I rely on the material being available, or do I have to book it?

If I am booking it, how long are the teaching periods so that I may have the equipment for as long as I need it?

Space

What kind of working space do I have?

Am I sharing it? With whom?

Do they teach in the same subject area, or are they teaching different subjects?

Are there areas in the space that might be dangerous?

Note: Who shares your space will have an impact on the ways you make your classroom welcoming, post student work, and so on.

Interference

How much interference will the bell/buzzer intercom system or phone likely cause?

What rules apply to cellphone use?

What interference may I expect from staff or other students?

What is the protocol for class interruptions?

Names

What are the names of the custodians, the secretaries, and my peers?

Pembroke Publishers © 2018 *Asking Better Questions*, 3rd ed., by Saxton/Miller/Laidlaw/O'Mara ISBN 978-1-55138-335-4

Getting Started: A Thinking Process for Teachers (continued)

School Policies

To avoid possible difficulties arising from the material you choose or the references you use, you may want to consider these questions:

What is the nature of the district I serve?

What is the school context in regard to the neighborhood — culture, ethnicities, religions, languages, dress and behavior codes?

What emergency procedures are in place?

Is there anything special I should know about the school or its environs? Who could I ask?

Support

What are the phone numbers of my own support system (personal and professional)?

Personal Attributes

What personal skills and attributes do I bring to my teaching?

What personal as well as professional goals have I set for myself?

How will I present myself to my students? (How will I talk? What will I wear?)

What sort of role model do I intend to be?

What is my attitude towards homework? Do I subscribe to the ideas that getting it done is the students' responsibility and getting it marked and returned promptly is my responsibility?

Relating to Other Staff and Administration

What are the special skills and attributes of my peers?

Do I feel able to ask for help when I need it?

Do I believe I should be self-sufficient?

How do I react to unsolicited advice?

Do I listen well?

Do I talk too much?

Am I ready to give a hand when asked?

Pembroke Publishers © 2018 *Asking Better Questions*, 3rd ed., by Saxton/Miller/Laidlaw/O'Mara ISBN 978-1-55138-335-4

Six Pack Shame by Linda Steele

The central image for Chapter 11

Evaluating Questions on Ann Graham

In Chapter 12, Session 4, the teacher asks students to evaluate the questions that were scribed during the in-role interviews. She hands out a response sheet to each group and gives students five tasks:

1. To look at the questions transcribed and decide what kinds of questions they are:
   - questions that elicit information — A
   - questions that draw out answers that fill in the gaps between the facts and help them make connections — B
   - questions that invite answers that deepen the story — C
2. To select three (or more) questions to examine closely
3. To determine the category of each question
4. To decide how each question chosen helps build the story
5. To consider whether the question could be rephrased in order to elicit a richer response and, if so, to rephrase it

> **Example 1: Mr. Taylor, what was your relationship with Ann's father?**
> *Question Category:* B
> *How did the question help us?* The fact that Mr. Taylor and Mr. Graham didn't get along made Ann's death near Mr. Taylor's farm more significant.
> *Rephrase?* Good question. Helped us find the plot line. No rephrase needed.
>
> **Example 2** (*to the barber*)**: You know a lot about what goes on in this village. Was Ann's mother a witch?**
> *Question Category:* A
> *How did the question help us?* It didn't. The barber only got upset that he was being called a gossip and refused to answer.
> *Rephrase?* Yes, option provided: There was a lot of talk about Ann's mother and her religious practices. I wonder if you heard anything that might help us understand what happened?

Note: If students are to analyze more questions than three, then provide each group with additional response forms.

Evaluating Questions on Ann Graham: Response Form

Members of Group: _____

_____

_____

- Question: _____

_____

Category _____

How did the question help us? _____

_____

Rephrase? Yes _____   No_____

Rephrase (if Yes) _____

_____

_____

- Question: _____

_____

Category _____

How did the question help us? _____

_____

Rephrase? Yes _____   No _____

Rephrase (if Yes) _____

_____

_____

- Question: _____

_____

Category _____

How did the question help us? _____

_____

Rephrase? Yes _____   No _____

Rephrase (if Yes) _____

_____

_____

Bibliography

Aker, Don. 1995. *Hitting the Mark: Assessment Tools for Teachers*. Markham, ON: Pembroke.

Anderson, Lorin W., David R. Krathwohl, Peter W. Airasian, Kathleen A. Cruikshank, Richard E. Mayer, Paul Pintrich, James D. Raths, and Merlin Wittrock. 2000. *A Taxonomy for Learning, Teaching and Assessing: A Revision of Bloom's Taxonomy of Educational Objectives*, edited by Lorin W. Anderson and David R. Krathwohl. New York: Longman.

Anderssen, Erin. 2016. "This Is Sabrina: Generation Z and the Future of Our Country." Focus. *Globe and Mail*, June 26, F 1, 3–5.

Appadurai, Arjun. 1990. "Disjuncture and Difference in the Global Cultural Economy." *Public Culture* 2 (2): 1–24.

Arnold, Roz. 1998. "The Drama in Research — and Articulating Dynamics." In *The Research of Practice/The Practice of Research*, edited by Juliana Saxton and Carole Miller, 110–31. Victoria, BC: Idea Publications.

Barnes, John. 1976. *The Writer in Australia: A Collection of Literary Documents, 1856–1964*. Melbourne, AU: Oxford University Press.

Barrett, Louise. 2005. *Beyond the Brain: How Body and Environment Shape Animal and Human Minds*. Princeton, NJ: Princeton University Press.

Bastock, Michelle, Brenda Gladstone, and Judy Martin. (2006–2007). "Inquiry Transforms Learning Environments for Students." *ATA Magazine* 87 (2): 27–29.

Berg, Maggie, and Barbara K. Seeber. 2016. *The Slow Professor: Challenging the Culture of Speed in the Academy*. Toronto: University of Toronto Press.

Berger, Warren. 2014. *A More Beautiful Question*. New York: Bloomsbury.

Berthoff, Ann. 1987. Foreword. In *Literacy: Reading the Word and the World* by Paulo Freire and Donaldo Macedo, xi–xxiii. South Hadley, MA: Bergin & Garvey.

Birkerts, Sven. 1995. *The Gutenberg Elegies: The Fate of Reading in an Electronic Age*. New York: Farrar, Straus and Giroux.

Blackburn, Simon. 1988. Interview. *Sunday Observer*, November 20.

Bloom, Benjamin. 1956. *The Taxonomy of Educational Objectives. Book 1: Cognitive Domain*. London: Longman.

Bloom, Benjamin, and David R. Krathwohl. 1965. *The Taxonomy of Educational Objectives: The Classification of Educational Goals. Book 1: Cognitive Domain*. New York: D. McKay.

Booth, Eric. 1999. *The Everyday Work of Art: Awakening the Extraordinary in Your Daily Life*. Naperville, IL: Sourcebooks.

British Columbia. School District No. 22. (n.d.). www.sd22.bc.ca abed publications.

Britton, James. 1970. *Language and Learning: The Importance of Speech in Children's Development*. London: Allen Lane.

Brookfield, Stephen D. 2015. *The Skillful Teacher: On Technique, Trust, and Responsiveness in the Classroom*, 3rd ed. San Francisco: Jossey-Bass.

Brooks, William Dean, and Philip Emmert. 1976. *Interpersonal Communication.* Dubuque, IO: W. C. Brown.

Brownlie, Faye, Susan Close, and Linda Wingren. 1988. *Reaching for Higher Thought: Reading, Writing, Thinking Strategies.* Edmonton, AB: Arnold.

Brummelman, Eddie, Stefanie A. Nelemans, Sander Thomaes, and Bram Orobio de Castro. 2017. "When Parents' Praise Inflates, Children's Self-Esteem Deflates." *Child Development* 88 (6): 1799–1809.

Bruner, Jerome. 1986. *Actual Minds, Possible Worlds.* Cambridge, MA: Harvard University Press.

Buber, Martin. 1965. *Between Man and Man.* Translated by R. G. Smith. New York: Macmillan.

Bunting, Eve. 1996. *Train to Somewhere.* New York: Clarion Books.

Burnaford, Gail E., Arnold Aprill, and Cynthia Weiss, eds. 2001. *Renaissance in the Classroom: Arts Integration and Meaningful Learning.* Mahwah, NJ: Lawrence Erlbaum Associates.

Caine, Geoffrey, and Renate Caine. 1994. *Making Connections: Teaching and the Human Brain.* Lebanon, IN: Dale Seymour.

Cambridge Advanced Learner's Dictionary, 4th ed. 2013. Cambridge, UK: Cambridge University Press.

Carrington, Victoria. 2017. "How We Live Now: 'I Don't Think There's Such a Thing as Being Offline.'" *Teachers College Record* 119 (12): 1–24.

Case, Roland. 2005. "Critical Discussions: Bringing Critical Thinking to the Main Stage." *Canadian Education Association* 45 (2): 1–8.

CMind (Center for Contemplative Mind in Society). 2015. contemplativemind. org.

Cohen, Jonathan. 2006. "Social, Emotional, Ethical and Academic Education: Creating a Climate for Learning, Participation in Democracy and Well-Being." *Harvard Educational Review* 76 (2): 201–37.

Cole, Ardith. 2002. *Better Answers: Written Performance That Looks Good and Sounds Smart.* Portland, ME: Stenhouse.

Damasio, Antonio. 1994. *Descartes' Error: Emotion, Reason and the Human Brain.* New York: Avon Books.

———. 1999. *The Feeling of What Happens: Body and Emotion in the Making of Consciousness.* Boston: Houghton Mifflin Harcourt.

———. 2003. *Looking for Spinoza: Joy, Sorrow, and the Feeling Brain.* New York: Harcourt.

Davenport, Coral. 2014. "Keystone Pipeline Pros, Cons and Steps to a Final Decision." Politics. *The New York Times*, November 18, A14.

Denzin, Norman K. 1997. *Interpretive Ethnography.* London: Sage.

Doidge, Norman. 2007. *The Brain That Changes Itself: Stories of Personal Triumph from the Frontiers of Brain Science.* New York: Penguin.

Doll, William. 1993. *A Post-modern Perspective on Curriculum.* New York: Teachers College Press.

———. 2008. "Looking Back to the Future: A Recursive Retrospective." *Journal of the Canadian Association for Curriculum Studies* 6 (1): 3–20.

Dunbar, Robin. 2002. *Grooming, Gossip and the Evolution of Language,* 2d ed. Cambridge, MA: Harvard University Press.

Dweck, Carol S. 2007. "The Perils and Promises of Praise." *Educational Leadership* 65 (2): 34–39.

Edwards, Derek, and Neil Mercer. 1987. *Common Knowledge: The Development of Understanding in the Classroom.* London: Methuen.

Edwards, A. D., and D. P. G. Westgate. 1987. *Investigating Classroom Talk.* Social Research and Educational Series 4. London and Philadelphia: Falmer Press.

Ferrara, Charles L. 1981. "The Joys of Leading a Discussion." *English Journal* 70 (February): 68–71.

Ferrett, Sharon K. 1997. *Peak Performance: Success in College and Beyond*. Chicago: Irwin Mirror Press.

Foer, Franklin. 2017. *World without Mind: The Existential Threat of Big Tech*. New York: Penguin.

Frederickson, Barbara L. 2001. "The Role of Positive Emotions in Positive Psychology: The Broaden-and-Build Theory of Positive Emotions." *American Psychologist* 56 (3): 218–26.

Freire, Paulo. 1970. *Pedagogy of the Oppressed*. New York: Herder and Herder.

———. 1974. *Education for Critical Consciousness*. London: Sheed & Ward.

Freire, Paulo, and Donaldo Macedo. 1987. *Literacy: Reading the Word and the World*. South Hadley, MA: Bergin & Garvey.

Frye, Northrop. 1988. *On Education*. Markham, ON: Fitzhenry & Whiteside.

Gardner, Howard. 1999. *The Disciplined Mind: What All Students Should Understand*. New York: Simon & Schuster.

Garrison, William H. 2003. "Democracy, Experience and Education: Promoting a Continued Capacity for Growth." *Phi Delta Kappan* 84 (7): 525–29.

Giroux, Henry. 1987. "Introduction: Literacy and the Pedagogy of Political Empowerment." In *Literacy: Reading the Word and the World*, by Paulo Freire and Donaldo Macedo, 1–28. South Hadley, MA: Bergin & Garvey.

Goldstein, Thalia R., Katherine Wu, and Ellen Winner. 2009. "Actors Are Skilled in Theory of Mind but Not Empathy." *Imagination, Cognition and Personality* 29 (2): 115–33.

Goleman, Daniel. 2006. *Social Intelligence: The New Science of Human Relationships*. New York: Bantam Dell.

Goodfellow, Robin. 2014. "Literacy Practice, Pedagogy, and the 'Digital University.'" *International Journal of Learning and Media: Formulations and Findings* 4 (3/4): 9–18.

Graves, Donald. 1983. *Writing: Teachers and Children at Work*. Portsmouth, NH: Heinemann.

Greene, Brian. 2008. *Icarus at the Edge of Time*. New York: Alfred A. Knopf.

Greene, Maxine. 1995. *Releasing the Imagination: Essays on Education, the Arts and Social Change*. San Francisco: Jossey-Bass.

Halverson, Erica Rosenfeld, and Kimberly M. Sheridan. 2014. "The Maker Movement in Education." *Harvard Educational Review* 84 (4): 495–504.

Harari, Yuval Noah. 2014. *Sapiens: A Brief History of Humankind*. Toronto: McClelland & Stewart.

Harris, Diane. 2006. "Open or Closed — That Is the Question." Paper presented at the annual conference of the British Educational Research Association, Warwick University, UK, September.

Hawkins, Thom. 1976. *Group Inquiry Techniques for Teaching Writing*. Urbana, IL: National Council of Teachers of English.

Homer-Dixon, Thomas. 2001. *The Ingenuity Gap: Can We Solve the Problems of the Future?* Toronto: Vintage.

Honan, Eileen. 2012. "A 'Whole New Literacy': Teachers' Understanding of Students' Digital Learning at Home." *Australian Journal of Language and Literacy* 35 (1): 82–98.

Hunkins, Francis P. 1974. *Questioning Strategies and Techniques*. Boston: Allyn & Bacon.

Ingram, Jenni, and Victoria Elliott. 2016. "A Critical Analysis of the Role of Wait Time in Classroom Interactions and the Effects on Student and Teacher Interactional Behaviours." *Cambridge Journal of Education* 46 (1): 37–53.

Janks, Hilary. 2012. "The Importance of Critical Literacy." *English Teaching: Practice and Critique* 11 (May): 150–63. http://education.waikato.ac.nz/research/files/etpc/files/2012v11n1dial1.pdf.

Johnson, Geoff. 2018. "Students Need Help with 'Alternative Reality.'" *Times Colonist*, The Capital and Vancouver Island, January 9, Section A, 8.

Kahneman, Daniel. 2011. *Thinking, Fast and Slow*. Toronto: Doubleday.

Kaku, Michio. 2018. "To the Moon, Mars and Beyond: Why Science Fiction Is Closer to Reality Than We Might Think." Opinion. *Globe and Mail*, March 3, 6–7.

Katz, N. 2016. "Your Brain on Devices: What the Media Says about Children and Digital Technologies," media release. *Federation for the Humanities and Social Sciences*, May 31.

Katzenbach, Jon R., and Douglas K. Smith. 1993. *The Wisdom of Teams*. Cambridge, MA: Harvard Business School Press.

Kim, James S., and Gail L. Sunderman. 2005. "Measuring Academic Proficiency under the *No Child Left Behind Act*: Implications for Educational Equity." *Educational Researcher* 34 (8): 3–13.

Konrath, Sarah H., Edward H. O'Brien, and Courtney Hsing. 2011. "Changes in Dispositional Empathy in American College Students over Time: A Meta-analysis." *Personality and Social Psychology Review* 15 (2): 180–98.

Kundera, Milan. 1986/1988. *The Art of the Novel*. Translated by Linda Asher. New York: Grove Press.

Kurfiss, Joanne Gainen. 1989. "Critical Thinking by Design." *Teaching Excellence: Toward the Best in the Academy*. (Autumn): 1–2.

Laidlaw, Linda. 2005. *Reinventing Curriculum: A Complex Perspective on Literacy and Writing*. London: Routledge.

Laidlaw, Linda, and Joanne O'Mara. 2015. "Rethinking Difference in the iWorld: Possibilities, Challenges and 'Unexpected Consequences' of Digital Tools in Literacy Education." *Language & Literacy: A Canadian Educational E-journal. Special Issue: A Landscape View of Literacy Studies in Canada* 17 (2): 59–74. http://ejournals.library.ualberta.ca/index.php/langandlit/issue/view/1684.

Laidlaw, Linda, and Suzanna Wong. 2016. "This Is Your Brain on Devices: A Close Reading of Media Accounts of Children's Use of Digital Technologies." Paper given at Congress of the Humanities and Social Sciences, Calgary.

Laird, G. 2010. "The Office of the President." *The Walrus* 7 (September): 42–51.

Langer, Ellen. 1997. *The Power of Mindful Learning*. Reading, MA: Addison-Wesley.

Luke, Allan, Jennifer O'Brien, and Barbara Comber. 1994. "Making Community Texts Objects of Study." *Australian Journal of Language and Literacy* 17 (2): 139–49. https://search.informit.com.au/documentSummary;dn=324756612074043;res=IELHSS.

Manzo, Anthony V. 1969. "The ReQuest Procedure." *Journal of Reading* 13 (2): 123–26.

Marsh, Jackie. 2017. "The Internet of Toys: A Posthuman and Multimodal Analysis of Connected Play." *Teachers College Record* 119 (120305): 1–32.

Marsh, Jackie, et al. 2017. "The Online and Offline Digital Literacy Practices of Young Children: A Review of the Literature." *COST ACTION IS1410*. http://digilitey.eu.

Michener, James. 1987. *Legacy*. New York: Fawcett Crest.

Miller, Carole, and Juliana Saxton. 2004. *Into the Story: Language in Action through Drama*. Portsmouth, NH: Heinemann.

———. 2015. "Developing the Capacity for Empathy." In *Drama, Theatre and Performance Education in Canada: Classroom and Community Contexts*, edited by Mindy Carter, Monica Prendergast, and George Belliveau, 10–19. Ottawa: Canadian Association for Teacher Education/Canadian Society for the Study of Education. Online.

———. 2016. "Mary Ellery: Traveler in Space." In *Into the Story 2: More Stories! More Drama!*, edited by Carole Miller and Juliana Saxton, 135–55. Bristol, UK: Intellect.

———. 2016. *Into the Story 2: More Stories! More Drama!* Chicago: Intellect.

Moffett, James, and Betty Jane Wagner. 1976. *Student-Centered Language Arts and Reading, K–13: A Handbook for Teachers.* Boston: Houghton Mifflin.

Moon, Jenny. 1999. "Reflective Writing: Some Initial Guidance for Students." https://www.cemp.ac.uk/downloads/resourcesforreflectivelearning.doc.

Moore, K., and J. McEwen. 1936. *A Picture History of Canada.* Toronto: Nelson.

Morgan, Norah, and Juliana Saxton. 1987. *Teaching Drama: A Mind of Many Wonders.* London: Hutchinson.

Napell, Sondra. 1976. "Six Common Non-facilitating Teaching Behaviors." *Contemporary Education* 47 (2): 79–82.

Neelands, Jonothan. 1984. *Making Sense of Drama.* Portsmouth, NH: Heinemann.

———. 1990. *Structuring Drama Work.* Cambridge, UK: Cambridge University Press.

Noddings, Nell. 2002. *Starting at Home: Caring and Social Policy.* Berkeley, CA: University of California Press.

———. 2005. *The Challenge to Care in Schools: An Alternative Approach to Education.* New York: Teachers College Press.

Ontario Ministry of Education Guidelines. 1988. Toronto: Service Ontario.

O'Sullivan, C. 2000. "The Shape of Things to Come: The Need for a New and Different Curriculum." Paper presented at 10th National Drama anniversary conference, York, UK, April.

Pahl, Kate, and Jennifer Rowsell. 2012. *Literacy and Education: Understanding the New Literacy Studies in the Classroom.* Los Angeles: Sage.

Parkins, Wendy, and Geoffrey Craig. 2006. *Slow Living.* Oxford, UK: Berg.

Paul, Richard, and Linda Elder. 2001. *The Miniature Guide to Critical Thinking: Concepts and Tools.* Dillon Beach, CA: The Foundation for Critical Thinking.

Perullo, Nicola. 2007. "Slow Knowledge." *Slow* 57: 16–21.

Petress, Ken. 2004. "Critical Thinking: An Extended Definition." *Education* 124 (3): 461–66.

Pinar, William. 1998. *The Passionate Mind of Maxine Greene: "I Am . . . Not Yet."* London: Routledge.

Postman, Neil. 1979. *Teaching as a Conserving Activity.* New York: Dell.

Powers, Richard. 2011. "Conditional vs. Absolute Learning: The Power of Uncertainty." *Stanford Social Dance.* http://socialdance.stanford.edu/syllabi/conditional_learning.htm.

Premack, David, and Guy Woodruff. 1978. "Does the Chimpanzee Have a Theory of Mind?" *Behavioral and Brain Sciences* 4 (4): 515–629.

Preston, Sheila. 2016. *Applied Theatre: Facilitation, Pedagogies, Practices, Resilience.* London: Bloomsbury Methuen Drama.

Ritchart, Ron, and David N. Perkins. 2000. "Life in the Mindful Classroom: Nurturing the Disposition of Mindfulness." *Journal of Social Issues* 56 (1): 27–47.

Rosenblatt, Louise. (1978) 1994. *The Reader, the Text, the Poem: The Transactional Theory of the Literary Work.* Carbondale, IL: Southern Illinois University Press.

———. 1988. *Writing and Reading: The Transactional Theory.* Technical Report No. 416. Urbana, IL: Illinois University. https://www.ideals.illinois.edu/bitstream/handle/2142/18044/ctrstreadtechrepv01988i00416_opt.pdf.

Rowe, Mary Budd. 1972. "Wait-Time and Rewards as Instructional Variables: Their Influence on Language, Logic, and Fate Control." In *Resources in Education*, Education Resources Information Center. Paper presented at the Association for Research in Science Teaching conference, Chicago, IL, April. http://files.eric.ed.gov/?id=ED061103.

Saul, John Ralston. 1995. *The Unconscious Civilization*. Toronto: House of Anansi Press.

Sax, D. 2015. "Ain't Nothin' like the Real Thing." *Globe and Mail,* October 29, A10.

Saxton, Juliana, and Carole Miller. 2015. "Developing the Capacity for Empathy." In *Drama and Theatre Education: Canadian Perspectives*, edited by Mindy R. Carter, Monica Prendergast, & George Belliveau, 10–19. Ottawa: Canadian Association for Teacher Education. Ebook.

Scardamalia, Marlene. 2002. "Collective Cognitive Responsibility for the Advancement of Knowledge." In *Liberal Education in a Knowledge Society*, edited by Barry Smith, 67–98. Chicago: Open Court.

Scriven, Michael, and Richard Paul. 2003. "Defining Critical Thinking." [for the National Council for Excellence in Critical Thinking Instruction]. http://www.criticalthinking.org/University/unibclass/Defining.html.

Sennett, Richard. 2012. *Together: The Rituals, Pleasures and Politics of Cooperation*. New Haven, CT: Yale University Press.

Shortz, Will. 2001. "How to Solve the New York Times Puzzle." *The New York Times,* April 8, n.p.

Siegel, Daniel. 2007. *The Mindful Brain: Reflection and Attunement in the Cultivation of Well-Being*. New York: W. W. Norton & Company.

Stahl, Robert J. 1994. Using "Think-Time" and "Wait-Time" Skillfully in the Classroom." ERIC Digests. http://files.eric.ed.gov/fulltext/ED370885.pdf.

Stein, Jess, ed. 1966. *The Random House Dictionary of the English Language: The Unabridged Edition*. New York: Random House.

Stiehm, Judith, and Bill Brown. 2002. *The US Army War College: Military Education in a Democracy*. Philadelphia: Temple University Press.

Strauss, Valerie. 2017. "The Surprising Thing Google Learned about Its Employees — and What It Means for Today's Students." *Washington Post,* December 20.

Sumara, Dennis J., Brent Davis, and Dolores van der Wey. 1998. "The Pleasure of Thinking." *Language Arts* 76 (2): 135–43. http://www.jstor.org/stable/41484086.

Tofade, Toyin, Jamie L. Elsner, and Stuart T. Haines. 2013. "Best Practice Strategies for Effective Use of Questions as a Teaching Tool." *American Journal of Pharmaceutical Education* 77 (7): 155–80.

Turkle, Sherry. 2015. *Reclaiming Conversation: The Power of Talk in a Digital Age*. New York: Penguin Press.

Vale, Ronald D. 2013. "The Value of Asking Questions." *Molecular Biology of the Cell* 24 (6): 680–82.

Vogt, Eric E., Juanita Brown, and David Isaacs. 2003. *The Art of Powerful Questions: Catalyzing Insight, Innovation, and Action*. Mill Valley, CA: Whole Systems Associates.

Wasserman, Selma. 2007. "Let's Have a Famine! Connecting Means and Ends in Teaching to Big Ideas." *Phi Delta Kappan* 89 (4): 280–97.

Weigler, Will. 2015. *From the Heart: How 100 Canadians Created an Unconventional Theatre Performance about Reconciliation*. Victoria, BC: VIDEA.

Whiteoak, Hannah. 2018. "The Importance of 'Wait-Time' in the Technology-Based Classroom." *Schoology*. http://www.schoolology.com.

Wiltse, Lynne. 2015. "Mirrors and Windows: Teaching and Research Reflections on Canadian Aboriginal Children's Literature." *Language and Literacy* 17 (2): 22–40.

Wolf, Maryanne. 2010. "Our 'Deep Reading' Brain: Its Digital Evolution Poses Questions." *Nieman Reports* (Summer). www.niemanreports.org.

Wu, Tim. 2016. *The Attention Merchants: The Epic Scramble to Get inside Our Heads*. New York: Knopf.

Zull, James E. 2002. *The Art of Changing the Brain: Enriching the Practice of Teaching by Exploring the Biology of Learning*. Arlington, VA: Stylus.

Index